*I went down to the moorings of the mountains,
The earth with its bars closed behind me forever,
Yet you have brought up my life from the pit,
O Lord, my God.*

Jonah 2:6

Dusty McLemore

LLBC Publishing

Gambling with Eternity: The Loser Wins!
Author: Dusty McLemore
© 2014 by Lindsay Lane Publishing
www.lindsaylane.org
All rights reserved.

This book or parts thereof may not be reproduced in any form, stored in a retrieval system, or transmitted in any form by any means without prior written permission of the author, except as provided by United States of America copyright law.

Cover Art/Photography: Lori Rigsby
Cover design & book design: Rhonda Martin - Martin Media
Co-writer: Brian Passe
Edited by W. Scott Moore, B.B.A., M.Div., D.Min. www.eleospress.com
Also available in eBook form.
Second print 2014.

Unless otherwise noted, all Scripture has been taken from the New King James Version®. Copyright © 1982 by Thomas Nelson, Inc. Used by permission. All rights reserved.

PRINTED IN THE UNITED STATES OF AMERICA

CONTENTS

Gambling with Eternity: *The Loser Wins!*

Foreword IX

Acknowledgements XI

Preface XIII

Chapter One: The Early Years 1

Chapter Two: Sweet Home Alabama 11

Chapter Three: Coming of Age 19

Chapter Four: My Testimony... 33

Chapter Five: Patsy's Testimony 47

Chapter Six: Round Island - My Seminary..................... 61

Chapter Seven: Family and God's Preparation 71

Chapter Eight: Called Out By God.................................. 85

Chapter Nine: Sharing My Faith 99

Chapter Ten: The Lindsay Lane Vision 125

Chapter Eleven: Worship, Serve, Grow 143

Epilogue 152

Bibliography.. 154

This book is dedicated to:

-My parents, Dempsey & Virginia — your lives have greatly encouraged me

-My lovely wife, Patsy — your unconditional love helped to lead me to accept Christ

-My Savior, Jesus Christ — Your sacrificial death has given me eternal life!

Foreword

I have often heard it said, " if you ever see a turtle on a fence post, you will know someone put him there." I love this story of Dusty McLemore because I have seen the finished product. It is apparent that God has done nothing less than the miraculous in this man's life, his marriage and his ministry. The Bible teaches that Jesus Christ is in the life changing business; as you turn the pages of this book you will see the miraculous unfold. The miracle of the Lord Jesus is not only what He did in history and what we read of from the past but what He continues to do on a daily basis. Dusty McLemore is nothing short of a miracle of God. For God to take a man who is living in rebellion to strategically, providentially and super naturally place people in his life that are there as a fence post, guard rail or even a sign post to point him to Jesus is glorious.

Read how God can take a man's life and literally change his destiny, how God can take a person with no real purpose in life and begin to give them meaning and direction that will make each day a day of celebration. To be able to live your life with meaning that comes as a result of what God did over 2,000 years ago on the cross.

For the Lord to take Dusty McLemore from where he was and to bring him to where he is today is interesting and inspiring. The most encouraging part is God desires to do the same with your life. You were created by a sovereign God who desires to have fellowship with you, to reveal His purpose and use you in His Kingdom agenda. All of this is possible in each person's life as a result of what Jesus did on the cross. As you read these pages you will see how that became a reality in Dusty McLemore's life. It will cause you to see our own poverty of spirit, mourn over our own personal sin and then watch God create a hunger and thirst in our soul for righteousness and for a Kingdom agenda. As you read this book you will be mindful of your own personal need or you will celebrate that the same thing has happened in your life and you will think of others to pass it on to. Each life will be richer for reading it.

I am grateful to God for the man Dusty McLemore, for his darling wife Patsy and his precious family. I am grateful for the work God did in him, through him and with him. His life, his family and his church is testimony that God took a man that was gambling with eternity and helped him to see that the loser wins.

- Dr. Johnny Hunt, First Baptist Church, Woodstock, GA.

Acknowledgement

Some special people who made this memoir possible:

Rhonda Martin has done the entire book design and layout; her talent gives the book its unique look that makes it easy to read.

This biography has been a long time in coming. It most likely would not have happened without the encouragement and trust of my dear friend, Brian Passe. He has labored faithfully in trusting God's direction.

I'm very grateful also for my loyal staff and church family! Together, they have constantly been a rock of support to me personally, to my family, and to my ministry.

To my precious family: you have stood by me through thick and thin, and seen the good, the bad and the ugly sides of me.

To my beautiful and godly wife Patsy: your resilience and trust in me are beyond my vocabulary. You truly are a virtuous woman!

Finally, I thank my God and my Savior Jesus Christ, who gave me life when I didn't want to live. He found me in the pit, and raised me up to His Pulpit as His Preacher! Jonah 2:6

Preface

In writing this book, I have been reminded just how blessed my life has been through Jesus Christ. I have been shocked to think where my life would have been today without Jesus Christ. He is my Savior, He is my Lord, and He is my King. Jesus Christ is my everything. As Jesus said, "Without the Father, I am nothing" and, believe me, without my Lord and Savior I am nothing.

There are two verses of scripture that have helped me along my journey. The first is 2 Corinthians 5:17, *"Therefore, if anyone is in Christ, he is a new creation; old things have passed away; behold, all things have become new."*

The second verse that has greatly helped me is 1 Corinthians 15:10:

> *But by the grace of God I am what I am, and His grace toward me was not in vain; but I labored more abundantly than they all, yet not I, but the grace of God which was with me.*

These two verses have greatly helped me to understand just who, and what, I am in the love of Jesus Christ. He is my Savior and my Redeemer; He has truly rescued my life from the pit. I still shudder to think of my life outside of Christ.

God's wonderful grace is so amazing. And, by the way, it still amazes me. It amazes me how God could take my life, with all the skeletons in the closet and all of my checkered past, and use me by placing me into His pulpit to proclaim to others the good news of the Gospel of Jesus Christ. Only our Lord could take a prodigal and make him into a preacher. That's why Paul wrote in 1 Corinthians 1:26-29:

> *For you see your calling, brethren, that not many wise according to the flesh, not many mighty, not many noble, are called. But God has chosen the foolish things of the world to put to shame the wise, and God has chosen the weak things of the world to put to shame the things which are mighty; and the base things of the world and the things which are despised God has chosen, and the things which are not, to bring to nothing the things that are, that no flesh should glory in His presence.*

God loves everyone. But God will choose even the down-and-out and the downcast. He will take anyone who is willing to call upon the name of the Lord, and He will use them for His glory.

It's true, my friend. If God can use my life, He can use anyone's life. God's love runs deeply—even to the deepest and darkest pits of degradation, defeat, and despair. By means of His great love He will not only find you, but He will also rescue you through His mercy and by His grace.

Corrie ten Boom, author of The Hiding Place,[1] wrote, "There is no pit so deep that God's love is not deeper still."

I am so very grateful to my God and Father for rescuing this sinner from the pit of despair.

My prayer is: that this book and my story will help to encourage you and remind you, my dear reader, of God's great love for you. Regardless of where you are, or where you have been, God's love has been freely offered to you—and to anyone who will call on the name of the Lord.[2]

---

[1] ten Boom, Corrie, John Sherrill, and Elizabeth Sherrill, *The Hiding Place* (Old Tappan, NJ: Fleming H. Revell Co., 1974).

[2] Romans 10:13.

ONE

The Early Years

I am so grateful for my parents, Dempsey McLemore and Virginia Dare Christopher McLemore, who raised me and my two siblings in a home environment where we felt loved, encouraged, and nurtured by parents who grew up very hard. My Dad was a firm disciplinarian, because he was raised that way with his brothers and sisters.

I would like to give you, dear reader, some insight into my Dad's journey in the military, and how he and my Mom met: June 6, 1944 is known as D-day. Thousands of men jumped into the blackness over France at 3:00 that morning. The thoughts of this young man from Alabama were overwhelmed by his new surroundings. He closed his mind to the noises and flashes of anti-aircraft munitions that were tearing both airplanes and gliders into pieces. My Dad's life was now measured only in terms of the next few moments—that's how long it would take for the brave members of the

82nd Airborne to reach the ground. They would begin a fight for survival that would last until morning's first light. For five days, my Dad and his fellow soldiers fought a frantic German army—an army that was being pushed back from the beaches of Normandy.

Finally, when he and his fellow soldiers ran low on ammunition, food and water, they had to either surrender or else be killed. Once captured by the German troops, they were placed into a series of forced labor camps.

The Allied forces constantly pushed forward. In response, the Germans moved the labor camp prisoners further into France and, then, into Germany. My Dad was eventually taken to a concentration camp in Dresden, Germany where, soon after his arrival, the Americans firebombed the city.

My Dad later told me (and I can remember this very vividly) how he and his fellow soldiers picked up the burnt corpses of men, women and children who were killed in the devastating bombing. In the closing months of the war, a Russian military unit liberated my Dad and the other prisoners that were being held in Czechoslovakia.

My Dad was part of a generation that God expected to carry forward every problem that He had placed upon them. It would take years for me to understand the fundamental truths that preserved our nation, and the way of life that I now enjoy.

My Dad loved my Mom; they had been dating before my Dad shipped out to Europe. Once freed from captivity, my Dad returned home eagerly to Alabama. He was processed out of the Army; he then traveled by bus from Norfolk, Virginia, to Decatur, Alabama. Once he reached Decatur, he hired a taxi to drive him fourteen miles to his home in Athens, Alabama. When he arrived, my grandmother, MaMa Mac, Daddy Mac (my grandfather), and all of the members of his family were filled with joy and relief.

My Dad was soon to be reunited with my mother in a very unique way. While driving to her workplace at the airport to surprise her, he topped a hill. He recognized the oncoming car as the one that would be taking her home after her day's work. He quickly pulled over to the side of the road, and ran toward the oncoming car. It was a climactic end to an incredible journey. Soon after, my Mom and Dad were married—on Sunday, September 2, 1945.

I am the youngest of three children. I have an older brother, Mike, and an older sister, Ginger. I was born on Saturday, December 5, 1952, at the Athens-Limestone Hospital. My Mom and Dad named me, "Oliver Dale McLemore." My grandaddy was Oliver Delmar and my Dad is Oliver Dempsey, so I became Oliver D. McLemore (III).

Soon after I was born, my mother gave me the

nickname, "Dusty." I once asked her why she called me Dusty. She said, "Well, I've always just liked that name" (I, however, figure it must have been because I was always getting into the dirt). That nickname has given me some troubles over the years—my passport lists me as "Oliver Dale," but my driver's license has "Dusty." On one occasion, as I was traveling abroad, I almost didn't make one of my flights. It was due to the confusion caused by my multiplicity of names.

I remember growing up in a family where there was always an abundance of joy. The world during my early years, however, was filled with many challenges and tribulations. My generation (the "Boomers") grew up during the "Cold War." We always expected the threat of nuclear attack and similar types of things.

I was two months old in 1953, when we moved to Aiken, South Carolina. The Atomic Energy Commission had contracted with DuPont to build and operate a facility for the production of atomic materials that would be used primarily for the purpose of defense. The DuPont Company was selected by the military to be its primary contractor. They hired my Dad to work for them and, so, we moved to South Carolina.

My Dad, a pipe fitter by trade, was employed to work in that capacity at the new plant. But, soon after we arrived in

South Carolina, he was moved to the operations division. He would now become a facility guard and, therefore, a federal employee. In his capacity as a federal guard, Dad was authorized to ticket people and, when necessary, to arrest them for violating federal laws.

My earliest memories of Aiken, South Carolina, were sitting in a swing set and watching my brother and sister go off to school. We lived in a trailer park that had sandy roads full of thistle-like spurs. Even so, we usually played outside in our bare feet. I remember having a white picket fence around our trailer.

Also, we grew up with a maid named, "Clorene." Clorene stayed with us while Mom and Dad went to work. Our trailer had plenty of room, but only one small heater. On cold mornings Mike, Ginger, and I would huddle in front of it for warmth.

During those early years, Kenny Wood was my best friend. His family lived in the same trailer park; we were both five years old when we met. Our playground was a small hill, where the soil was loose and sandy. It was much different from the red clay to which I have now grown accustomed in Alabama! Our favorite game was playing with toy cars, pushing them through the dirt.

Kenny and I were playing outside one day, when I hit his head with a rock. He started bleeding badly. That day my Dad gave me the worst spanking I have ever received! Mom got mad at him for whipping me in anger; Daddy just shrugged her off; he said it was, "strong discipline."

Our family camped most weekends at the Clark Hill campground in South Carolina. My Dad had a wooden Yellow Jacket boat, about fifteen feet long, with a thirty-five horsepower Johnson motor. He loved to fish for bass, a trait that he passed on to me. Dad would get off work before my Mom and, since I wasn't in school yet, I would go with him to the campground to set up camp. When Mom got off work, she, Mike, and Ginger would join us at the campsite.

I remember that Mr. and Mrs. Smith frequently joined us at the campground. The Smiths had become friends with Mom and Dad shortly after we moved to South Carolina. My Mom and Dad were both great water skiers; we spent much of our time swimming, tubing and skiing.

Dad loved to fish and hunt. But, since he was a true family man, he chose to share his passion for sports with his family. Every Friday, before the others arrived at the campsite, Dad and I would fish by ourselves. It was usually dark by the time he got the boat in the water, so he would always put a pallet under the bow of the boat for me to sleep.

One of my favorite memories is the time my Dad caught a large fish that got away. As he and I were fishing near a brushy shoreline, Dad hooked a big, large-mouth bass. As he held the bass up to put it in the live well, it jumped out of his hands. Off balance and reaching for the fish, Dad and the bass both fell out of the boat and into the water. It was a shallow area, and so he was able to stand up in the weed bed. This time I wasn't asleep. I just stood there as he climbed back into the boat. What a memory that event has etched into my mind!

The most memorable thing that happened while we lived in South Carolina was the time when we were kicked out of the trailer park. While I was still in diapers, I got into a fight with the owner's son! During a childish disagreement that eventually became physical, I bit him so hard that he cried all the way home. His Dad, carrying a big stick, brought his son back to our trailer. He handed the stick to his son, and demanded that he hit me with it. He was yelling loudly, "Hit him with it! Hit him!" His loud shouts awakened my Dad.

My Dad's temper would sometimes flare up, and it surely did that day. He charged out of the trailer, jumped the white picket fence, and punched the owner in the face. You couldn't really call it a fight—that one punch finished it. Although the fight ended our family's time at that trailer park, I think my Dad would say it was worth it!

I started first grade at the New Ellenton Elementary School in South Carolina; I finished that year at the Reid Elementary School in Alabama. Before we left South Carolina, however, I had met my first love. Her name was Sylvia Tippy Droughty, and she was in the second grade. I wanted to give her a unique gift to show my "love" for her. I searched my sister's jewelry drawer to find a necklace that I thought Sylvia would like. I placed it into a box, wrapped it in black electrician's tape, and gave it to her in the lunchroom the next day. I sat across the table from her. I watched as Sylvia unwrapped the gift. She showed it to everyone.

When Ginger first asked where her necklace was, I told her I didn't know anything about it. Later, I felt guilty. I admitted to her that I had given it to Sylvia. Although Ginger was furious with me, she let Sylvia keep the necklace. She didn't want me to be embarrassed. Ginger has always been a good big sister!

Our Dad was, and still is, close to each of his three children. Our Dad is a man of exceptional physical strength. He is also a man of firm discipline and commitment to his family. His love for us, however, has always been "sprinkled" with his foundational values. These values, or core beliefs of his heart, have been absolute throughout our childhood years; his rules were not to be broken.

Growing up, I loved my father but I feared his discipline. I did not take much comfort in the fact that my Dad's discipline applied equally to all of his children. I just wanted to have fun, so I would avoid his spankings at all costs!

Ginger is the oldest of the three children, and Dad's only daughter. The bond between a father and daughter can probably only be understood by a daughter and her father (as I've learned with my own two girls). Ginger and Dad continue to live to this day with that unique bond.

My brother, Mike, and I learned from our Dad how to be men; it has taken many years for me to fully understand all the things he has tried to teach us. He would let us, as young boys, explore life in our own ways—but under his rules. Mike and I would frequently fish or hunt with Dad. Those times we spent with him gave us the opportunity to listen to, and watch, this man of exceptional character. Dad's early lessons have made a difference in both our lives.

My brother and sister's paths have been different from mine, but our links to Dad and his character have never broken. Someone has said, "A father is his son's hero, and his daughter's first love." That is so true with all of us!

TWO

Sweet Home Alabama

New job opportunities drew my Mom and Dad back to Alabama, where my grandparents owned acreage in the town of Reid (just outside of the city of Athens). In 1960, we moved our trailer from South Carolina, and parked it next to MaMa and Daddy Mac's house. We lived in the trailer for about a year—until our new house had been built.

My great-grandfather, grandfather, and Dad had all lived, at various times, at the old home place. As the oldest son, my Dad was given the first rights to purchase the land. The new house, built on this land, was where I grew up. Mom and Dad live there to this day. We consider this to be our "home place." We laughingly call it, "McLemore Hill."

Electricity and indoor plumbing now come standard in every new house. That wasn't the case for Daddy and MaMa Mac's house. They had a traditional outhouse, and drew their water from a well.

Their neighbors, Lice and Mary Ann Yarbrough, also had an outhouse. I remember they used Sears and Roebuck catalogs for toilet paper! Lice and Mary, an elderly African-American couple, were like family, so Daddy always took care of them. Their property didn't have a water supply, so they would come and draw water from MaMa Mac's well. Eventually, Daddy ran water lines to their house so they could have indoor plumbing. My Mom and Dad have always helped others who were in need.

My Dad and his brother-in-law, Fred Christopher, formed a partnership. They opened a Standard Oil service station business. It was a "full service" station—where you could buy gas, have your car fixed, or drink a cold Coke. For me, it was the place where I would go regularly to either fill my bike tires with air or put a patch on an inner tube. If you lived in Athens at that time, you may remember seeing their gas station—at the corner of Jefferson Street and Highway 72. It was eventually torn down. It has been replaced by the Taco Bell restaurant that is still operating there to this day.

My Dad and uncle expanded their partnership to include a company named, "Christopher Insulation." I was twelve years old when they started this new venture; my brother, Mike, was sixteen. The two of us were immediately "drafted" into the insulation workforce.

The process of insulating houses required someone

to crawl into an attic. This person would have to carry a large hose that they would use to direct the insulation that would be blown in from the hopper. Another person, on the ground, would feed bags of insulation into the hopper. That insulation would always cling to your clothes! Mike and I would often help to fill the hopper, while Dad would crawl into an attic by himself.

Alabama summers have always been hot and muggy; working in those conditions required that we would drink a lot of water. We also needed frequent breaks from the oppressive attic heat.

One day, Daddy didn't come down as scheduled. Mike and I became concerned, so we climbed into the attic, where we found him passed out from heat exhaustion. We called for an ambulance, and they took him to the hospital. He was cooled and rehydrated for several hours. Fortunately, Dad recovered completely; he was able to return to work the next day.

The service station and the insulation company were both profitable businesses. They both eventually grew to the point that my Dad and my uncle decided to dissolve their partnership. My Dad became the sole proprietor of the insulation business; my uncle became sole owner of the service station.

Daddy would buy his insulation in Mount Pleasant,

Tennessee. I would often go with him to help load the truck. The route would take us north through Pulaski and, then, into central Tennessee. There were no interstate highways along this route, so we would travel the back roads through some of Tennessee's most beautiful countryside.

My Dad saw other opportunities for financial growth, so he sold the insulation business. He joined with my mother's uncle, Aaron Shannon, in a fish bait and tackle business.

They raised worms on Aaron's farm. In the summertime, my cousin and I were assigned the task of picking worms out of the worm bed. We would turn up the soil to locate the worms; we would then count out fifty worms to a container.

Dad traveled a lot in those days. He would "make the rounds" to the small country stores that sold his bait and tackle supplies. His routes took him to places such as Tuscumbia and Florence, Alabama. Sometimes, I would ride with him. These were special times, when we were able to talk—and to just be together. Some of my happiest memories are from just riding with Dad as we traveled the back roads of northern Alabama.

When Dad worked in the bait and tackle business, he always had plenty of lures and fishing equipment. We were able to continue going on our fishing trips, just as we had in

South Carolina. One memory I'll always hold dear is a time when Dad's route took us to the west side of Tuscumbia, Alabama. It was a long, but very enjoyable, day. We stopped at a trout farm. Dad asked if I wanted to fish for trout. The farm owner provided a fishing pole, and we used corn as bait. That night, we had fish for dinner! Momma took the four trout I had caught earlier that day, added French fries and hush puppies, and fed the whole family.

No matter how hard his day had been, or how busy he was, Daddy always wanted to know what I had been doing and thinking. Each of us kids knew that we were our parents' top priority. Whenever they were able, they attended the different events that each of us was involved in.

As I mentioned earlier, both of our parents taught us a strong work ethic. Our small farm was large enough for Daddy to plant cotton and to raise farm animals. Although Daddy had a full-time job, he always worked a few hours on the farm before dinner. Every morning, he told Ginger, Mike, and me what chores had to be done that day. He was absolutely firm that all chores would be completed on time and according to his instructions before any play. No excuses would have been accepted.

Like Daddy, my Mom also had a full-time job. When she got home from her work at night she went straight to work, either on the farm or in the house. My parents' work ethic was normal to them; we learned ours by the example they gave us.

One summer, Mike and I got one of our most memorable chores on the farm. Not wanting the cattle to roam off the property, Dad built a fence around the pasture. He first made a string line, and then placed posts at equal distances along the line. Our job was to dig the postholes! Every morning, Dad gave us a daily quota of holes to dig; Mike and I knew it would be best to meet that quota.

Unlike today, when you can rent auger machines, Mike and I dug each hole with a manual posthole digger. The soil in northern Alabama is rich in nutrients, clay, and limestone. Clay and limestone were dauntless problems for two young boys. We would have paid anything to be anywhere but along that fence line. Once our posthole-digging job was finished, Dad would give us a new job—paint each post! Dad's nature was to work hard. He always did his best on every job. Also, he was very committed to being precise (whether or not I thought it was necessary). For instance, if you were to drive by our house, you wouldn't have seen the house or the fence because the trees surrounded it. That didn't matter to my Dad as he aligned the fence's path with a string. If the posts were not exactly along the line, we would have to dig new holes.

I once said to him, "Dad, we're in the back forty. Nobody is going to see this fence." His only response was, "But I can see it." I am so grateful for all the times when he said, "Son, if you're going to do it—do it right."

One summer, Dad and three of his friends built a camp at Beulah Bay on the Tennessee River. In addition to the camp, they built a houseboat and a pier with a metal frame. Our families spent many weekends at the camp and on the houseboat. We used the campsite until I was a senior in high school, when TVA[3] issued a new set of rules that allowed only floating piers to be built along the river. Dad and his friends removed the pier and sold the houseboat, thus ending our camping weekends.

Dad often took Mike and me crappie fishing near the camp. We went to an area full of tree stumps, shallow enough for Dad to wade in and pull Mike and me in the boat. He didn't have to do that—it was something he wanted to do in order to teach us about being a loving family. While the pier and houseboat are gone, their special memory remains in my heart.

I had a great childhood growing up in sweet home Alabama. I'll never forget those vivid memories of fishing and hunting with my Dad, swimming in the creek behind our

----

[3] The Tennessee Valley Authority, "a corporation owned by the U.S. government [that] provides electricity for 9 million people in parts of seven southeastern states at prices below the national average."

house, or playing army in the pines with my cousins.

I have wished, many times, that my children and grandchildren could experience the life I lived on our farm. Those are memories I still cherish, and will never forget.

THREE

Coming of Age

Life has many challenges. We face them individually, as families and even, sometimes, as a country. My parents grew up the hard way, and yet they persevered. Both of their fathers fought during WWI; both sets of their parents raised their children, for several years, during an economic depression.

The WWI generation of parents sadly watched as *their* children went off to fight yet another world war. Many of their children would not return home to raise a family.

I did not live through the hardships experienced by either my grandparents or my parents. My tribulations would come, but certainly not with the intensity that they had endured. When I look back, I can see how I came to be where I am today. There were many times when my tribulations would blind me. However, there were also many joys that have helped me to persevere. My parents taught me discipline, commitment, and hard work. In their world, quitting was never an option. But, ultimately, they allowed me to make my own decisions. I was allowed to choose to either live by the values they had instilled in me—or not.

One of the earliest personality traits I developed was my competitiveness. Although this has been an area of strength, I have also discovered that it has become one of my greatest weaknesses. This competitive spirit would one day bring me close to the point of death. Not as an athlete on the field of play but, rather, as a broken man in a closet crying out for help.

I loved to participate in all sports; I still have fun on the golf course, competing with my friends. Today we may laugh, taunt, and cheer each other on, but ultimately each of us still wants to win!

I was about eight years old when my Dad took me to my first Little League baseball tryouts. They did not have different leagues for particular age groups like they do today, so my Dad took me to the town of Tanner. His best friend, Harold Stacy, was a coach. I remember Dad asking him if there would be a place for a left-hander. And that became my introduction to organized sports.

I loved watching and playing baseball. My favorite team was the New York Yankees. They played in the 1961 and 1962 World Series. The games, at that time, were always

Coming of Age

played in the daytime.

Those two summers, 1961 and 1962, I picked cotton with my Uncle Bobby. At noon, we would go home for lunch. My uncle would turn on the radio so we could catch part of the games. I remember three Yankees in particular: Mickey Mantle, Roger Maris, and Yogi Berra. All were famous, and very good players. I listened to them on the radio and, sometimes, I even got to watch them on television. That ignited my passion for the game, and motivated me to play and compete at my very best.

I played center field, because that was the same position where Mickey Mantle played. Because I was left-handed, my high school coach wanted to move me to play first base. I told him that I didn't want to play in that position—I preferred the outfield. I wanted to become the next Mickey Mantle.

In football, my hero was Joe Willie Namath. He wore the #12; that was the number I wore, as well. Just like Joe Willie, I was the only player on the Tanner High School football team that wore white cleats! I played as a quarterback and as a receiver because my best friend, Kent Murphy, was an all-star quarterback. He started ahead of me at that position so, as a senior, I played mostly as a wide receiver.

After the football season, I played basketball. "Pistol Pete" Maravich became my basketball idol. He could do wonders with a basketball, and was ahead of his time in the sport. I learned to dribble between my legs and behind my back, the same way he did. It's amazing how sports figures can have so much influence upon a child's life.

My passion for sports and competition would eventually foster something within me that would lead to another passion: gambling. On football game days, during my senior year, the varsity team would stay in the gym until game time. The coaches would lay out mats so the team could rest. But my friends and I preferred to play cards usually for dimes and quarters. There were no large bets, because we were resting and only doing it for fun.[4]

Gambling became so compelling to me that, one summer while picking peaches at a local orchard, my cousin and I bet on the style, color or model of the next car that would drive by on the four-lane close to the orchard. It was just a way to pass the time but, actually and honestly, I would have done anything to compete and to gamble.

My involvement in sports got me out of doing a lot of chores, while Mike and Ginger stayed at home. However, things began to change in 1969. Ginger got married, Mike joined the Air Force, and Dad's job took him to North Carolina for six months. Now it was only my Mom, the farm and I. Even though Dad would come home on some weekends,

---

[4] Actually, I was doing it to win; I loved the high that came with winning. It didn't need to be anything important or valuable. I just loved to win.

I had to "step up" and work the farm in his place.

That was not the easiest thing for a teenager, but it did have some exciting moments. I'll never forget the time when Mom and I helped birth a calf. As the cow struggled to give birth, Mom and I became frustrated—we didn't know how to help her. Our only hope was to contact Dad by telephone. He told us, "You will have to pull it out." We had never done this before, so I just grabbed one hoof and Mom grabbed the other. We had to wait until the cow pushed and, when she did, I put my leg on the cow for leverage. Then we pulled the calf's legs. Finally, we pulled the calf out. The calf just lay there for a moment, until it finally started to breathe. We cleaned it up and, within a few minutes, it rose to its feet and walked away.

It was during this time that I stopped attending church. I had been baptized at the age of twelve during a week of Vacation Bible School. I really enjoyed the youth group, and had a few close friends. But, at the age of sixteen, I decided to walk away from church. It no longer interested me. I started out skipping a Sunday service once in a while. Finally, I just stopped attending altogether. Mom continued to attend but, at that time, I joined with my Dad in staying at home.

Leaving the church placed me among many worldly influences—with some severe consequences. I have no way of guaranteeing that, if I had not left the church, I would not have started to gamble. However, I am certain that, without church fellowship, I became extremely vulnerable to the world's pleasures and its resultant sufferings. I can say, with certainty, that worshiping and serving in the fellowship of a church will give you far more strength for living your life than if you try to live in the world without the church.

Even though I had stopped going to church, I still believed in God. Once I started getting more focused upon sports and girls, I pushed church attendance to the side. I also started running with a different crowd of guys.

In eleventh grade, I started making friendships with people who were older than I was. Some of them were out of high school; I started hanging out and drinking with them. That had a significant influence upon my life.

My new circle of friends did not attend church, either. It may sound strange now, but I don't remember people in my high school talking openly about Christ. No one ever talked about his or her faith!

One of the main reasons I intentionally focus on our youth today is because I do not want them to experience what I did in school. I tell them that I admire them, because they are focused on Christ at a young age. I want our youth to know that I didn't have a relationship with Christ at their age, and that I truly admire them for their spiritual maturity.

I take every opportunity to encourage them to speak openly about Christ. If we do not spread the message, who will?

The year 1971 was a turning point for me. It was when I first met Patsy Jo Holland, and had secretly started dating her!

I graduated from high school that year, and started attending Calhoun Community College. I had planned to major in Physical Education. I wanted to coach sports, where my competitive spirit could have an outlet. Life was good in 1971. It could only get better![5]

I worked with my best friend David at the Greenbrier Cotton Gin in the fall of 1972. We worked from 6:00 p.m. to 6:00 a.m., Monday through Friday. Our job was to pull cotton trailers, loaded with cotton, to the vacuum for processing into bales. After work we would first eat breakfast, and then we would return to John C. Calhoun College for classes. It was at the gin where I first met and placed a bet with a bookie. My friend knew the bookie, so he invited him to the gin to meet me. He gave me the game sheets that listed the teams and point spreads for the next week. I studied the sheets, and then selected the college teams to bet on. That weekend I won $200! This was too easy, and I loved it!

If you're not a gambler, you may not know that sport gambling is extremely technical. It is not just a matter of betting on your favorite team. The bookie knows what he is

---
[5] This would also become the time when I began placing bets with bookies.

doing, and has a lot of experience. Believe me, he's not in it to make friends, or to help people make money. His goals are to win, and to separate you from your money!

The bookie's game sheets included professional and college games. When you placed a bet, you didn't just bet on who would win the game. You also had to "give points" or "take points." I studied the newspapers to see who had home field advantage, the most injuries, and which teams were ranked the highest. The bookies knew all of this, too, and they understood all of the ins and outs.

Gambling was easy, in the beginning, when I was fresh and full of vigor, and before a looming debt developed over my head. That fall, I thought I was invincible. Some of my friends began to call me, "easy money!" The year ended on a high note: I had won some money, and Patsy and I were seeing each other a lot!

It's kind of funny how Patsy and I first met! When I first checked her out, my intentions weren't entirely noble. I was dating her best friend at the time. I thought I could make my girlfriend jealous by asking Patsy out for a date. Patsy accepted, and we agreed to meet at a basketball game. I thought Patsy was sixteen (since that was my girlfriend's age). Patsy was beautiful, and very mature—but only fourteen! (Her maturity came as the result of taking care of the house and her two brothers, Max and John.) I almost fainted when I found out that she was just fourteen!

She also told me that she was not allowed to date. So, if I wanted to see her again (and I did) I would need to meet her at ball games or at parties. At first, since her parents didn't know we were dating, I couldn't pick her up at her home. They found out after a couple of months; I then started visiting her at home. I was allowed to take her out on double dates when she turned fifteen.

Over the next two years, my gambling increased—and so did the risks. Also, as my gambling increased, I started to cut my college classes. I had signed up for easy courses so I wouldn't have to study. Because of gambling, I eventually quit college. I needed a job to support my gambling habit and to pay my losses. I lost $200 on the 1973 Super Bowl game, and I didn't have a penny to pay the bookie. Nor did I have a job! So I had to take out a $200 loan to pay him. My brother-in-law, "Pig Iron," went to the bank with me to cosign for the loan.

In 1973, I started working part-time at the Helena Chemical Company. I also told my folks that I did not want to go to college. Once free from college, I began to work full-time at Helena. With extra time and money, I began to focus more on playing softball and gambling. Patsy knew that I was gambling, but I was able to hide the extent of it from her.

In March of 1973, I asked the question that would transform my life in ways only God could know. I asked Patsy Jo Holland to be my wife. At the time, she was sixteen and I was twenty.

Patsy and I do not advocate marriage at such a young age! I often tell parents that, back then, it was like the days of Mary and Joseph: couples married when they were younger! They never buy that one! The inexperience and immaturity of youth places an enormous strain on a marriage. And, at a young age, we are often blinded by our wants and self-interest.

I finally got up the nerve to ask her parents if I could marry her! We told both of our families that we were getting married; no one objected—*except* her father! He finally relented, however, and came around to the idea on the day of the wedding!

At that time, there was no way for me to have known that God had a plan for Patsy and me. It would be many years before we would realize how close our lives had come to disaster, and how God's providence had saved both of us from ourselves.

We were married on July 20, 1973, at the Bethel Church of Christ in Athens. It would be six years before either of us would enter a church on a regular basis.

Patsy quit high school, earned her GED,[6] and then at-

---

[6] The General Educational Development Test, a high school equivalency certificate.

tended cosmetology school. I worked full-time at Helena. We purchased a new trailer as our first home. Life seemed great. We had jobs, steady incomes, and a host of friends who also loved "the party scene." Weekends were something we lived for. I played in a semi pro baseball league, and Patsy went to the games with me on weekends. Parties, baseball, gambling and a wife—I had it all. The Bible says that wisdom and knowledge come from a fear of the Lord. Not for me! The only people I feared were the bookies (and that was only if I lost a bet).

Over time, Patsy's awareness of, and anxiety from, my compulsion to gamble began to grow. I assured her that it was under control, and that I was making a lot of extra money for us by gambling. I handled all of the finances; this made it easy for me to conceal any heavy losses or loan payments from Patsy. By this time, I was employed at Monsanto Chemical and making more money.

One day, when Patsy was in our car, she found two payroll checks from Monsanto that I had forgotten to deposit. I always had money in my pocket from playing poker. It wasn't really greed for money that drove me; it was the high from competing against the bookies—and winning!

One particular week, I won five thousand dollars. I brought all the money home—in cash. I'd never seen so much cash! I showed Patsy the money and placed it on the kitchen table. I positioned one hundred dollar bills on the outside perimeter of the table in a large circle. Next, I placed all of the fifty-dollar bills in a circle inside of the hundreds. I followed suit with the twenties, tens, and fives. I used our Polaroid camera to take a photo of all that money on the table.

I couldn't wait to show all the guys what "The Big Cheese" had done! I carried the picture to work that night. I passed it around the break room for all to see.

Having lots of money can make you feel like you're somebody, but it can also give you a false sense of security. I remember that I used the winnings to buy Patsy a diamond ring (to pacify her); I bought myself a pickup truck.

Though I won a lot of money, I was still losing to the bookies. In gambling, the house always wins! I had one particular and memorable loss: I was playing billiards one day. I forgot that I had placed $350 in cash in my shirt pocket to pay the bookies. After I had left the pool hall, I discovered my pocket was empty. I went back into the pool hall; I asked if anyone had found $350. No one spoke up. Duh! I was so mad and sick that I went home and called Monsanto. I told them that I wasn't coming to work! I was too sick! And I was. Sick of myself!

One day, in 1975, Patsy informed me that she was pregnant. Though she did not drink during her pregnancy, we did not stop attending our weekend festivities. There were still ball games to play and parties to attend.

That summer, while we were partying on the river, Patsy was eight months pregnant with Haley. My cousin and his wife, along with another couple, joined us to water-ski. Suddenly, a black cloud formed over the Tennessee River, preventing us from getting to the shoreline. We had been drinking and, with youthful enthusiasm spurred on by alcohol, we stood up on the sides of the boat. The waves lifted us high above the water. One wave came over the boat; it flooded the motor, while we were about one hundred yards from the shore. We were floating in the river—with a flooded boat and a dead motor. Fortunately, the boat did not entirely sink, leaving us stranded in the middle of the river. The top of the boat, however, was flush with the water line; the gas tank was floating beside the boat. We put on life jackets and held onto the boat as we dragged it toward the shoreline. Once on shore, we found some cans and bailed out the boat. Luckily, my cousin was able to start the engine. He then drove the boat out onto the river, pulled the drain plug, and drained the water by speeding across the river. By this time, we were near the Tennessee Valley Authority nuclear plant. We faced a long, bumpy ride back to the dock. The water was so rough that I became worried about the possibility of Patsy having an early delivery!

Patsy delivered our first little girl, Haley, on August 25, 1975. While we both expected the baby to be a boy, we fell in love with her the moment she was born. I now faced new responsibilities: a mother and daughter needed a husband, and a father. I wasn't prepared for all that would be involved with a new baby. But, like so many parents, we forged ahead—learning as we went along.

Probably because of my competitive spirit and my love of sports, Haley grew up to be a "tomboy." But Haley took on the challenge! She became very good at sports—especially softball.

The next four years were not comfortable ones for our family. My gambling grew more out of control, and the strains of raising a child grew along with it. Looking back, I believe it was all part of God's plan for both Patsy and me. While my gambling was pulling my family apart, God's conviction in Patsy's life was holding us together. We were not aware of God's plan at the time. Looking back, however, I can now see how God used those four years to get us where He wanted us to be.

However, we would first have to go through the fires of challenge and tribulation.

FOUR

My Testimony

My brother, Mike, received his college degree from Samford University in Birmingham, Alabama. In January 1979, he was in his final year of school at the New Orleans Theological Seminary. He and his wife, Wanda, had worked hard to prepare for the ministry. My parents, my sister, her husband, "Pig Iron," Patsy, and I all went to visit them on January the first.

For me, visiting Mike in the "Big Easy" was the perfect opportunity to see Alabama play Penn State in the 1979 Sugar Bowl for the National Championship. Patsy and I, along with our friends Larry and Jeanette, had driven separately, because we planned to party and attend the Sugar Bowl. Of course, I had a $500 wager on the game; that just added to the thrill of watching Alabama play! It was the year for what has now become known as the infamous "goal line stand." In the final minutes of the game, with Alabama leading 14 to seven, Penn State was at the one-yard line. If they had scored, I would have had to pay $550 to the bookie. Alabama's defense stopped them for four plays in a row! Bama won, and so did I! Life was good.

Or was it? By the summer of 1979, my gambling *habit* had become a compulsion. Gambling was now controlling my life; it was ruining my marriage and my family. Just juggling our finances and keeping secrets from Patsy created an enormous amount of anxiety. I was living from week to week, alternately winning and losing. I was so addicted that I was betting on everything. I made wagers on horse racing (something I knew nothing about) and also on boxing. During the NFL strike, I even placed a bet on our local high school football team.

I knew that I was addicted, but I would never admit that fact to anyone. Patsy knew I had a gambling problem and begged me to stop. I just laughed it off. I assured her that I knew what I was doing. I really wanted to quit, but I wasn't ready to admit it yet. The pull of my addiction was so strong that it was fooling even me. By this time, I was regularly receiving loan payment coupon books in the mail. I'd pay off one loan on a "good" week, and would take out another loan on the next week. At that time, it was fairly easy to go to the independent loan companies to take out a loan, and I was getting good at it. I kept thinking that I could win the money back because I'd done it so many times before. Deception was growing to another level.

On one particular day, Patsy and I met our friends at Point Mallard in Decatur for some "fun in the sun." Before we left home, however, I must have let my guard down: I forgot to get the mail out of the mailbox, so I let Patsy bring it in. That day, she found a coupon book filled with three years' worth of payment slips. Needless to say, we argued all the way to Decatur. She pointed out that we were living from paycheck to paycheck, her car couldn't be trusted to get her back and forth to work, and I was making payments for what God only knew or for how long.

At the same time, we began to receive phone calls and letters from creditors. I was even receiving threatening calls from my bookies! Again, my philosophy was that I would win the money back. Now I found myself in a desperate situation. I knew I was way out of my league. Even the bookies were concerned about my out-of-control betting. They had gone so far as to cut me off from betting for a few weeks until I could catch up on the money I owed them.

At this point, the thrill of gambling was gone. Money no longer had any meaning! The power and aura it had given me vanished, and I finally knew the truth. My life was in a downward spiral, and I actually wanted to stop gambling. My wife was threatening to leave me if I didn't quit and, like always, I promised her I would quit and seek help. She, however, had heard it all before—the lies, the promises, and the deception.

I knew my compulsion had such a grip on me that I couldn't stop on my own. I tried to convince myself that all I needed was one solid week of not gambling in order to get myself together again. However, even then, deep down inside I was thinking about how I was going to win it all back. Picture in your mind two little friends on your shoulder, one of them telling you, "Get a grip and stop this insanity." On the other shoulder, a little guy is saying, "Are you kidding? You can do this. You've done it before." My pride took over and I continued to gamble.

Patsy lived with a lot of stress; she was also under spiritual conviction. She was dealing not only with an irresponsible husband but, since Haley's birth four years previously, she was also convicted about her failure to meet her responsibilities for Haley. She was now attending the church where we were married—the same church where her parents were currently members.

Something was happening inside of Patsy, and she didn't even realize it. The joy of being married to me wasn't as much fun anymore. She began to view Haley as an underdog, (since her mother was not being responsible). Going to church on Sunday mornings was becoming an outlet of relief for her. Our married life was not what she had envisioned six years earlier—and she was scared! She was concerned for herself and for our little girl—and for *me*.

Finally, on a Wednesday afternoon in August 1979 (just before I was to leave for the second shift at Monsanto), she gathered her courage. She came to me and said, "I'm going to church tonight! I'm going on Sunday morning and on Sunday evening, and I'm taking Haley to church with me!" I didn't understand what she was telling me by that statement, but I knew she meant what she had said. She started going to church every time the doors were opened. Something had happened inside of her! I didn't know what it was, but it didn't take long for me to figure it out. Her life was changing right before my eyes![7] She stopped nagging me about quitting my gambling; she even stopped drilling me about where I had gone and what I had been doing. I watched her closely, waiting for her to either fall or to mess up.

One day, Patsy told me to sit down. Rather, she *commanded* me to sit down.[8] She exclaimed, "Dusty I can't keep living this way. Haley deserves a better mother than I've been. I've given my life to Jesus! I love you, and I want you to get right with God also, but I can't do that for you. I've turned you over to Jesus."

Looking back, I can now understand that she didn't fully

---
[7] The Bible calls it, "Peace that passes all understanding."
[8] In the vernacular, "She sat me down."

understand that salvation had come to her through God's grace. But, then, that's what's so amazing about God's grace, we don't have to learn it all we just have to submit to it. And that's what she did. But, that would be a whole new book that we could write!

Deep down, I wanted what she had. But I had too much pride to say it. In my mind, by having tried and failed to change my gambling habits, I had already lost my chance to get right with God. That hadn't worked; I felt hopeless. I had sworn that I'd never be like all of those hypocrites— they lived one way on Sunday, and another way the rest of the week. I was now completely miserable, but Patsy *wasn't*; that made me become even angrier. But I knew this Jesus stuff was real. How could you fight that? What I didn't realize was that the same God that had created the universe and had begun a work in Patsy was also busy working out a plan that would bring Dusty McLemore down—and win my heart forever. And He was using my wife to do it!

Nearly three months had passed. Things were quickly coming to a head. In October of 1979, our home and family lives had become a pressure cooker. I had been gambling daily for eight solid years; I knew something had to change. But how would it happen? I couldn't imagine my life without gambling. My mind went back to default mode. I thought, "I can control my life! I'll just win it all back." But, for the first time in all my years of gambling, I was about to panic. I was in debt way over my head. The bookies that had once always welcomed me were now making threats upon my life. I owed them thousands of dollars. They were telling me, "We want our money and, if we don't get it soon, we know where you live." They threatened to start collecting on the debt by breaking my arms and legs.

I was twenty-seven years old. I knew they were serious. How could something that had given me so much pleasure in the past now be turning and destroying my life? However, that's the way that sin works. Just like any other addiction, gambling had run its ugly course in my life.

After I became a Christian, I heard a wonderful, dear man of faith, Adrian Rogers, say, "First, sin thrills, and then it kills; sin fascinates, and then it assassinates." How true that was in my life. I now think, "Why couldn't I have learned that principle before now?" But, then, I clearly know the answer to that question.

I was miserable and wanted off this vicious "merry-go-round." All I knew to do was what I had done many times before. I could "double up to catch up!" That had been my motto in times past when I was having a losing streak. But the stakes had never been this high before!

I had another bookie that I could only contact through a private number. When I called him, I would use my own personal identification number that he had assigned to me. My number was fifty-seven. In an attempt to catch up, I made the call. "Hello, this is fifty-seven," I began. "I need to place some bets this weekend. I know I already owe you a lot of money, but I have access to some money, and will settle up with you next week." As usual, I was lying—I had mastered the art of that sin.

"Okay, fifty-seven," the voice on the other end of the phone line said. "But, you know you had better come across with our money—or else." I knew what the "or else" meant.

I proceeded to bet a few thousand dollars on some college football games. I had studied the particular match-ups closely. I had done background reports on each team's injuries, home field advantages, and scores from the previous season, along with many other statistics. I felt good about my bets. Normally, watching a sporting event after I had placed a wager was the ultimate high. It was like watching the Super Bowl every week! But this time that wasn't the case.

The bets were called in and set. I had wagered on ten college games that Saturday. Unlike the first time when I had placed a bet with the bookies years ago, this time I lost eight out of ten games. Now I was even more depressed. All I knew to do was to try and catch up again by betting on pro football on Sunday. And so I did.

I called my bookies once again. I made a desperate appeal to them to allow me to place another series of bets. Finally, they agreed. I was in so deeply now that I had lost all sense of reality. I just wanted out. I desperately needed to win. Sunday came. I picked my teams. But, just like on Saturday, I lost five of the seven games.

Now I *truly* began to panic! What would I do? How would I pay these guys? In my confused mind, all I could think of was Monday Night football. That would be my one last chance to win back not only the money, but my life as well!

On Monday evening, October 30, 1979, I called the bookies. I pleaded with them to let me place one last bet. I told them, "Win or lose, this is it." Also, I once again promised them that I had access to some quick money. I said, "I'm settling up and getting out."

I thought, "But, what if I were to lose? What in the world will I do?" I was extremely nervous; the stress was almost unbearable. For years it had been so exciting and fun. But, now, my addiction was about to destroy everything that I cherished. I thought about my wife and my daughter. I also thought about my parents. What would *they* think of me if they knew what I had become? My life flashed before my eyes, as I frantically waited for 8:00 p.m.—and the Monday night football game.

The Atlanta Falcons were playing the Seattle Seahawks in Atlanta's Fulton County Stadium. Atlanta had a chance to make the playoffs; they were favored slightly to win. My bet was on Atlanta. They would need to win by at least three-and-a-half points. The first half was very close, so I was a nervous wreck!

At halftime, I went outside and into my garage. I prayed to God. I told Him that, if He would allow me to win this game, I would quit gambling and start going to church. I really thought that I meant it but, deep down in my heart, I knew myself all too well. Would I, or *could* I, ever stop gambling?

I went back inside. The game was close, all the way to the end. After Seattle faked a punt and scored a field goal, they were leading by three points. There were only a few minutes left to play. Atlanta was driving the ball down the field for a winning touchdown. That's all I would need to win the bet and my life back. They reached the twenty-yard line, and were driving hard for the goal line.

I remember vividly the following series of events. Atlanta's quarterback, Steve Bartkowski, dropped back to pass; I was certain he would score. He probably could have run for a touchdown but, instead, he elected to throw the ball into the left corner of the end zone. Suddenly, a Seattle defender jumped up and intercepted the ball. Game over. I lose!

My heart sank deeply into my chest. I almost kicked in the television screen! I remember going outside and just staring into the night sky. I thought, "What will I do? How will I pay the bookies?" I was frightened by the thoughts of suicide that were running wildly through my mind. The evils of gambling had run their course. It had now destroyed my life. The choice I had made, so many years ago, to gamble had now haunted me beyond measure.

As my wife and I lay in bed that night, she knew that something was terribly wrong. I told her that I owed a lot of money (she had no idea either how much I owed or how desperate the situation really had become). I couldn't believe that she was still staying with me after all the hell that I had put her through.

My life, lying there in bed, was playing out before me on the darkened ceiling. Thoughts of suicide were now forming into a plan. I considered, "How can I stop all of this pain? How am I going to do it?" I thought to myself, "If only I had listened to my wife and others when they tried to tell me where my life was headed."

I had always thought I was in total control. But, now, I had made a complete mess of my life! I recalled Patsy's faith in Jesus Christ, and how strongly it had grown. He had given her such great peace through it all. I began to think of what she had told me about how much Jesus loved me, and how He had died for my sins.

Around 3:00 a.m., I couldn't deal with the pressure any longer. Out of sheer desperation, I got out of my bed. I walked over to our closet, fell on my knees, and began to weep profusely. Crying out in desperation, all I can remember saying was, "God, save me! God, save me!" I repeated it over and over again. I didn't know how God would do it, but I was certain He could do it. I had witnessed what He had done for Patsy.

As I prayed, I immediately experienced the Spirit of God coming into my life. It was like the weight of the world had been lifted off of my shoulders. At that moment, I knew that I had been saved! Something drastic had happened inside of me. Suddenly, I felt the loving arms of my dear wife around my neck. We embraced as we wept together. She had entrusted me to God, and He had come through for her. I remember telling Patsy, "I just got saved! I just got saved!"

I didn't understand it then but, later, I came to realize that God had answered the prayer I had prayed in my garage that night. But He had chosen to do it His Way! I can now admit that, if I had won that Monday night game, I probably would still be gambling. God knew that, too. He loved me enough to allow me to get to the end of myself!

God had saved me, and delivered me from my sins. Yet the consequences of my sin would still left be left behind for me to reckon with. I still owed the bookies a lot of money. But, now, I would have a vast peace inside of me to help me through any circumstance or situation that I would encounter. God was now in control!

My wife and I just sat there on the closet floor. We wept. But the tears of remorse had now turned into tears of joy. We both knew that God had changed our lives and our home. We could now face the consequences, together, as a team. With both God and Patsy by my side, I felt that I that could face any circumstances that I would encounter in my life. My wife had never given up on me! She had displayed the faith that it had taken for tough love to prevail.

I was working a swing shift at Monsanto at that time. My work hours enabled me to call my mother later that morning to tell her that her son had been saved. I knew my Mom had been praying for me a long time, so I couldn't wait to tell her the good news about my salvation. However, I also realized that I would have to tell her about my gambling.

She was elated to hear about my salvation experience. When I told her about my compulsive gambling habit, and how that God had delivered me, she said that I'd have to tell my Dad. I asked her to tell him for me, but she refused. She said, "It's now time for you to 'man up,' and to take responsibility for your actions." I waited until late in the day for Dad to return home. My father wasn't a man of faith at the time but, when I explained the depths of my problem, he immediately helped me secure a loan from the bank. I paid on that loan for three-and-a-half years! It was like making another mortgage payment—all while we were living in our little trailer. However, it was worth every penny. It was there, at the very rock bottom, where I looked up and saw Jesus with His open arms.[9]

My last telephone call that day was to my bookie. I explained what had happened—that I was now saved. I told the bookie that I would need a few days to secure the loan and to pay him. Fortunately, he agreed to wait for the money. Once I had paid him, I was fully free from the addictive power of gambling!

This, again, is a perfect example of God's amazing grace: to be totally delivered from a nine-year-long addiction in the twinkling of an eye. Amazing! Yes. Amazing Grace!

---

[9] Matthew 11:28-30.

FIVE

Patsy's Testimony

On March 14, 2012, my wife, Patsy, gave her testimony at Lindsay Lane Baptist Church. This would be the first time I had ever heard her complete testimony. This is her side of our story:

My testimony is so closely related to Dusty's that, I feel, I am being redundant by mentioning parts of it. He's always taken the blame for so many of the problems we have had in our marriage.

I was like a child, running with an older crowd and trying to be big and fit in. I have felt I was the luckiest person in the world to have been married to Dusty McLemore. I was also highly vulnerable, because I was insecure. I had no self-respect. I was a co-dependent accident, waiting for a place to happen.

I wasn't raised in church. My family started going to church when I was in middle school. After we moved to

Athens, AL, from Montgomery, Momma met new friends and wanted to start going to church. When she asked Daddy to go with her, he said, "Yes, but only to a Church of Christ." That was fine with Mom—it made no difference to her which church they attended as long as they went somewhere. You see, my Dad, as a young boy, was raised in the Church of Christ; my Mom was raised in the Nazarene church.

When I was twelve years old, I did what almost every twelve-year-old in church will do: I walked the aisle and got baptized. I had a real desire to please God. In my mind, I had done it. I felt good about myself for a long time. However the older I grew, and the more I became involved with friends in school, the more I was tempted to sin. My brother was a year older than I; I hung out with the kids in his grade. Before I knew it, I was right back where I had started. "Being a Christian" didn't feel good anymore, so I was baptized again when I was fourteen. But nothing changed. I remember thinking, "The only way I can go to heaven is if I die while asking for forgiveness for my sins."

I was with some friends two months before my fifteenth birthday. One of them was going to her boyfriend's house. That's the day I first met Dusty. He was *her* boyfriend! It wasn't long before he became interested in me. I didn't know it at the time, but he was using me to make his current girlfriend jealous! After a short time, this cat-and-mouse game was over—we were going out together. Our problem was that, since I was only fourteen, I was not allowed to date! At first, I didn't tell Dusty how old I was. I just lied and schemed, and sneaked out to see him.

My Dad worked a lot. My Mom was going to school and working the second shift as a nurse. That meant I didn't have much parental supervision. By this time, temptation had moved to a whole new level. But it didn't faze me spiritually anymore—I was in love! I had replaced my desire to please God with a desire to please Dusty. It bothered me at first, because giving myself to someone so completely was not what I had really wanted to do. However, I had to make a choice. And I made it!

Dusty graduated from high school in 1971, and started college in the fall. I, on the other hand, was only starting the ninth grade! By the spring of 1973, I was finishing tenth grade, Dusty had dropped out of college, and we were making plans to get married. I left East Limestone High School—and never looked back. We were married on July 20, 1973, and moved to Dusty's hometown of Reid, Alabama.

In 1974, I passed the GED exam, and started attending cosmetology school. At first, it seemed as if I was playing the role of a child, with Dusty as the Daddy. The problem was evident: he wasn't any more mature than I was. We were just having fun playing house!

In January of 1975, I came down with what I thought was a terrible bug. I was so tired I couldn't hold my head up. It didn't take long for me to figure out the "problem"—I was expecting our first baby! Haley Nicole was born on August twenty-fifth of that same year. When I saw her for the first time, I knew right away that she was going to be a game changer. Dusty and I loved our tiny baby girl, Haley, more than anything else in the world.

As she grew older, I began to remember how I used to care about what God had thought of me as a child. Now, however, I realized that I wasn't a child anymore! I was an eighteen-year-old mother—feeling as if I was going on thirty. Was it really time for me to grow up and become the Mom?

I started back to church, and took Haley with me. I would always invite Dusty to go with us; he'd visited my church while we were dating. He didn't want to go back. It may have pleased my parents that I was going to church, but it didn't really change anything. I was just living like a hypocrite. The older Haley grew, the harder it was to have fun doing the things that Dusty and I had been doing.

Of all of our mutual friends, only one couple had children. As a result, we were taking full advantage of our parents' willingness to keep Haley on the weekends so we could party. Haley was well taken care of, so no one was being hurt—except for me. And the fact that God was convicting me!

Like many young girls, I had made a vow that, when I would have children of my own, I would be a better mother than mine had been. It's so easy to see the mistakes your parents have made with you but, at this point in time, I began feeling that God was calling in my promise.

I truly wanted to do the right thing. I wanted to be a good mother, a good wife, and a good Christian. My problem was that I knew I would have to make some hard choices. Before, the choices hadn't been that tough. But, now, I had a little girl to think about. I was responsible for her. I knew I couldn't trust Dusty to change.

Finally, something happened that would rock my world. It would help me to realize that, if I didn't step up, it would be Haley who would suffer. There was a woman in my church who was quite a bit older than I. She had a little girl about the same age as Haley. She was a well-respected professional, and affluent enough to provide well for her child. The truth is that I was jealous of her, and ashamed of myself for not being what I should be.

One Sunday, as I was taking Haley to Sunday school, the woman stopped me in the hall. She told me that Haley would be going back to her old class because her new class had become overcrowded. In her words, she said, "Since Haley doesn't come all the time, she can stay in her old class." This lady never knew how much she hurt me that day. But God eventually used that pain to open my eyes. I was finally able to see that *other people* were not hurting Haley—I was.

From that moment on, I never stopped thinking about my relationship with God. I knew something was going to change. I didn't know when or how, but I knew it would happen.

Our home had become a boiling pot in early summer of 1979. Haley and I went on a vacation with my Mom and Dad to see my grandparents in Missouri. We were gone for almost two weeks. This, in my mind, would be a time of separation from Dusty! Maybe he would miss us terribly and change. But, instead, I was the one who became homesick. I quickly knew that this wasn't the answer. Also, I had an extremely strong conviction about divorce. I would rather have asked God to end my life than to have failed in my marriage.

Let's fast-forward a couple of months. Haley turned four years old on August 25, 1979. For her birthday, we had bought her a metal swing set. Dusty and I tried to put it together before her party, but he was not really strong on patience. He also refused to read the directions! Before he finished, he was cussing a blue streak. He was throwing nuts and bolts everywhere. It struck me, at that point, that I was living my life in much the same way as he was trying to assemble the swing set—without God's directions. I had been following my own directions! I went into the house. I fell apart, crying, and said: "Lord, I give up."[10]

At that time, my understanding of God had been that He was a deity in heaven. He was looking down at me, waiting to see me mess up—so He could squish me like a bug. I'd never been taught that I could have an intimate love for, and personal relationship with, Him. A few days earlier, I had been talking to God, trying to make arrangements with Him to fix my mess. Now He was telling me, "The only way you're going to get this right is if you give up!"

One Wednesday morning, I told Dusty, "I'm going to church tonight." He just looked at me as if to say, "Well, all right." I had never gone to church on a Wednesday night before. I said, "I'm going on Wednesday nights, Sunday mornings, and Sunday nights—and every time the church is open. I'm going to change something. Haley and I are going to follow God. I love you, Dusty, and I want you to go with us. But that will have to be your decision."

I did not have one ounce of security as I spoke those words to him. Our whole marriage was volatile, and my life was a mess. I didn't know whether Dusty would kick me out or leave me. That was the amazing thing about it: at that

---

[10] I honestly don't remember if we ever finished the swing set that day.

very moment, when I had declared to Dusty that I was going to stand with God, the Holy Spirit came into my heart. He empowered me to do things I had never been able to do before. From that moment on, *everything* changed. And I mean everything changed! I know it sounds cliché, but the peace of God came over me. There is no other explanation for what happened to my life that day! I had been living in constant turmoil. I couldn't sleep at night. My life had been a wreck, and I had been full of guilt about my little girl. I had felt responsible for her. Sadly, what I had told Dusty that night seemed to have no effect on him.

I started going to church, and I stuck to it. At that time, I was still attending the Bethel Church of Christ. A revival was being held there shortly after I started going again. That week, I walked the aisle. I rededicated my life to Jesus. That's what I called it, and it was like a miracle to me.

Three months after my "rededication," Dusty accepted Jesus Christ as his Lord and Savior.[11] That night, October 30, 1979, neither of us could sleep. Suddenly, I heard Dusty speaking, with a broken voice, in the closet. I didn't know what was happening. Then I heard him begin to cry. Weeping, he cried out, "Save me! Save me!" At that very moment, I got up out of the bed. I walked over to join Dusty in the closet. I wrapped my arms around him.

Dusty had often said to me, "I'm sorry. I won't ever do

---

[11] See "Chapter Four: Redemption - My Testimony" for Dusty's version of these events.

it again. Please forgive me." In fact, I had heard him say that so many times, and for so many years, that I no longer believed him. That night, however, when he said it, I could tell by his tears that this was real. I didn't have any doubts in my mind.

Although I didn't question his decision (I knew that it was real), Dusty and I were still destined to follow different paths. After Dusty was saved, he and I chose to attend separate churches. Whereas he went back to his home church (Round Island Baptist), I continued to attend services at the Bethel Church of Christ.

I was saved. I had no doubt in my mind about it. I had walked the aisle. I had wanted to live the right way; the Lord knew I was trying. I knew that God had saved me. The Holy Spirit had come into my heart—I never doubted that. He was clearly changing the way that I was living my life.

However, Dusty and I soon discovered that the two denominations differed on certain critical doctrinal issues. Those differences made for very difficult times in our lives and in our home. I was so bound by what I had been taught. My view of God was that He was extremely legalistic. But, in spite of that, I was still grateful to Him; I knew that He loved me.

At this point, I started digging into the Word. I needed some answers, and I was determined to find them. I was sincere, and God knew it. The point is: God knew my heart. He knew where I was in my spiritual walk.

Dusty and I started doing what he has said in his testimony.[12] We debated, we argued, and we screamed! If you had looked into our window at that time, you never would have believed that we had just been saved. We would brawl over the Bible.

It was not about who was right or wrong—and neither of us was winning. I don't know if Dusty understood that at the time. He thought that I was attending Bethel because my parents were there, and because I had been there most of my life. Also, he thought I was just being stubborn, and that I would never leave that church. I don't know at what point he came to realize that I was sincerely devoted to God, and that I was unwilling to do anything out of disobedience that might cause me lose it if I let it go.

To prove that to Dusty that I wasn't going to Bethel Church of Christ because of my parents, I switched my membership to the Tanner Church of Christ. I didn't know anyone in that church. I didn't realize it at the time, but this would be just another appointment God had with me. The ladies at church mentored me in becoming a godly wife. It wasn't about which church that I attended; it was about how to be a good wife to my husband.

---

[12] See "Chapter Four: Redemption - My Testimony" for Dusty's version of these events.

Patsy's Testimony

On a typical Sunday morning, Dusty and I were preparing to go to our separate churches. Haley would be, once again, caught in the middle, pulled back and forth between the two churches. As I walked out of the house, and onto the front steps, I asked Haley if she would like to go with me to my church. She started to cry. She said, "I don't know what to do. I don't want Daddy to be mad at me, and I don't want you to be mad at me, either." I told her, "Honey, I'm not going to be mad at you. You don't have to worry about that. You go with Daddy. You're going to be fine."

I got in the car and, as I drove to church, I prayed, "God, will you please just take my life? Take me out of here, and take me out of the equation. Then everything will be okay." Well, He didn't. And so I went on to my church.

I didn't plan on doing this but, on that Sunday, I spoke to a dear man who was an Elder at the church. I told him that I needed to leave the church. He was already aware of the fact that I had been visiting at Round Island with Dusty on some Sunday nights. He also knew my home situation, and my predicament with Haley. I said, "I don't know what to do—but I can't keep doing *this*."

I got into my car and started home. I prayed, "God, I know you have been using Haley since she was born to draw me to Yourself. I don't believe for one second that You want this to happen in her life. You know my heart as a mother, and that I love her so much. She's such a precious gift to me. I can't do this anymore. You just have to understand."

I didn't understand what I was doing. In my mind, I didn't know what I might lose, but I had to do what I was about to do. I went home. I told Dusty, "Okay, I give up. I'll go to church with you." However, when I went to Dusty's church, I went with my arms tightly folded—I didn't want to allow anyone to get into my heart.

I was back in my routine of pleasing Dusty again; at least that's what it felt like to me. This had been going on for a few years; I now felt that it was essential for the future our marriage that things would have to change.

I went to Round Island and, to my surprise, those people started loving on me. At first, I felt like an outsider—everything they did was foreign to me. The members' fellowshipped with each other. They actually talked to each other when they were outside of the church.

Dusty and I began to do things with some of the other couples from the church. We were always sociable, only now we were doing things together with other Christians. Even so, in the back of my mind, the doctrinal principles I had learned in the Church of Christ were staying with me.

One morning, I felt myself being drawn away from the Church of Christ. I remembered the warnings: "This is *what* will happen, and this is the way it will happen." I felt that I was being drawn away from my church as I was going over to become a part of this other group of people.

Dusty had already gone to work, so I was at home, alone, with Haley. It was the first time, in days, that it had not been raining. The clouds were still blocking the sun. I said to the Lord, "God, will you show me something that will tell me whether I'm doing the right thing or the wrong thing? Will you just give me a sign?" I was asking Him for something that I considered to be impossible, because I wanted to know for sure. I asked, "God, will you just allow a beam of sunlight to break through these dark clouds? Would you just show me your light?" And what did he do? He sent the most beautiful beam of light through the clouds that morning! I still have a picture of that event in my mind, because it was His answer to me.

From that moment on, I realized that many of the things that I had been taught were not true. I started to fall in love with God, because He had given me a new chance. He had set me free!

It didn't come all at once. It was a process—He knew I couldn't take it all in at once. I had been living a seriously legalistic life.

I don't believe I could have persevered if God hadn't intervened in the way that He had. He was so patient and merciful with me. He's done nothing since, but show me His mercy and grace.

I don't know for whom I have written these things. But it was for someone. God has told me that it was.

SIX

Round Island—My Seminary

Seminary, for me, began at my home church: Round Island Baptist Church in Athens, Alabama. Most people probably wouldn't think of going to church as attending a seminary. I do believe, however, that the people of Round Island both discipled and educated me to become a pastor.

Shortly after I was saved in October of 1979 at the age of twenty-seven, Pastor Karl Johnson baptized me into the membership of Round Island. He had visited me once in my home while I was still gambling; three months later I was saved. His visit, while not welcomed at the time, both intrigued and convicted me. Why would someone like Karl visit with, and pray for, someone like me? I have never forgotten his visit. And, certainly, I will never get over it, either!

After I was saved, and because of Karl Johnson, I decided to go to Round Island. It was also due to the fact that it was the church in which my Mom, my sister, and her husband were active members.

My brother, Mike, had moved to Birmingham, Alabama, and Daddy wasn't going to church at that time. Some people were still going to the church that had attended with me when I was younger and growing up. I felt that God was leading me back to Round Island. But Patsy kept going to the Church of Christ!

I went to Sunday school the very first Sunday when I returned to Round Island. There was a Bible in an empty chair; they told me to sit in that chair. I asked, "Whose Bible is this?" They told me, "It's yours." To this day, I do not know who gave me that Bible. But I still have it, and I cherish it. In that Sunday school class, I knew I was loved. And, as a class, they immediately started mentoring me. My first Sunday school teacher was Gene Russell; he still attends and teaches Sunday school at Round Island.

I was now totally committed to church. I knew that God saved me, and I, unconditionally, wanted to be there to grow and learn.

The church presented a program on Sunday nights, called "Training Union." I would study my lessons and attend the classes every Sunday night. The classes, though similar to Sunday school classes, were in a much more practical format.

Round Island—My Seminary

As I became more acclimated to the church, I began to grow in my commitment to the Lord. I became very active in the church. I was eventually asked to take on several different leadership roles. The first year after I was saved, I accepted the position of Training Union Director. This was one of my first roles as a servant in the church.

On a typical Sunday night, we would meet first in the Sanctuary. As the Director, I would give a devotional message. Although I had been active for a year, I was still nervous when I stood in front of the congregation, presenting my ten-minute message.

The next role I was offered, and accepted, was the position of Sunday School Superintendent. I began this new duty about six to eight months after I had accepted the role of Training Union Director. Man, I thought this was so neat! To think that God would use me to teach and to lead others!

On Sunday mornings, all of the Sunday school class members would first gather in the Sanctuary. I would present any administrative changes, as well as give them a devotional overview of the lesson. After these devotions, everyone would go to their Sunday school classes. I was now holding two leadership roles in the church!

In my second year at Round Island, the church members invited me to become a deacon! The process included a personal interview with all of the local Associational Pastors and leaders, as well all our deacons at Round Island. I remember being as nervous as an alley cat! The process felt more like an interrogation than an interview! Anyway, I must have passed the exam—the church ordained me to become one of their new deacons in May 1982.

I later learned that the primary roles of a deacon were to support our pastor, help serve the church, and take the lead in organized events. Another important duty of the deacons was to visit the older members of the church before deacon meetings.

I'll never forget how Ms. Norton always made sugar cookies for our visits. As a result, every deacon wanted to visit with her.

Once our visits were completed, we would return to church for our deacons' meeting. I remained as a deacon at Round Island for eight years; I even served as the chairman for a couple of those years.

One thing I honestly enjoyed at that church was singing in the choir. Sometimes, I would be asked to sing a solo. I would always say, "Yes." And then I would almost have a heart attack, singing in front of all of those people!

I also wrote a few songs about my new life in Christ! John Willet, an elderly gentleman who attended Round Island, would always hang his hat in the foyer. He would also

Round Island—My Seminary

give chewing gum to the children. When he passed away, I wrote a song about him that I sang at his funeral. Here are a few of the lyrics:

> *Are you sleeping, are you sleeping, Brother John, Brother John?*
> *John has gone to Heaven,*
> *John has gone to Heaven.*
> *Hallelujah, Hallelujah,*
> *There's a hat hanging in the foyer*
> *In the back of the church*
> *It belonged to a friend of mine.*
> *He was old and grey,*
> *But in his own way,*
> *Boy, didn't he shine.*

Round Island eventually changed the format of its Sunday night classes to topical studies, with times for discussion. I was asked to teach one of the adult classes. Each week I would teach a lesson on a particular topic. That's when I first began to realize that God was confirming His calling upon my life to become a preacher of the Gospel! He was stirring something inside of me that I had known had been there for a while. I knew that he was calling me to preach, but I didn't want to admit it. As a matter of fact, I shuddered at the thought!

During a fall revival service at Round Island, God

powerfully placed His hand upon me to preach the Gospel! John Karl Davis was the visiting evangelist. His sermon on Sunday night was, "Will God Burn Your Barley Field?" The message was taken from 2 Samuel, chapter 14. David's commander, Joab, wouldn't allow David's son, Absalom, to speak with King David. As a result, Absalom later rose up in opposition; he rebelled against his father David. Absalom had previously told Joab, on a number of occasions, that he had wanted to see his father. Joab kept dragging his feet. He would tell Absalom that he would arrange it, and then he just ignored the request. Absalom finally burned Joab's barley field in order to get his attention.

It was during that service that I would come under unbelievable conviction! That Sunday night, John Karl Davis asked, "What's it going to take for God to get your attention? Will God have to burn your barley field?" At that moment, I honestly thought that God might take my daughter, Haley, in order to get my attention so that I would yield to His call to preach.

Prior to this particular night, I had gone to see my brother, Mike. I had asked him how he knew when God called him to preach. I had also gone previously to talk with my pastor, Bill Bailey. I had informed him that God was calling me to do something, but I didn't know exactly what. He told me that God was probably calling me to preach. I replied, skeptically, "No, it couldn't be that." And then I asked, "How do you know what He's calling you to do?" Pastor Bailey told me that if I believed I was called to do anything else, then I should do it. That was very wise advice!

The fact that I was under conviction was something I really didn't want to admit. That Sunday night, as John Karl Davis preached his message, I said to myself, "What's it going to take for you to surrender to God and preach?"

By this time, God had been dealing with me for several months. He had been calling me to follow the path He had set for me. I thought to myself, once again, "Would He have to take my daughter or do something drastic to me? Would God really burn my barley field in order to get me to surrender to preach?" That night I was under such firm conviction that I couldn't sleep.

John Karl Davis preached during another revival service on Monday night. That was the evening, in August of 1991, when I walked the aisle to surrender my life to preach God's Word. I walked humbly and directly to my Pastor, Bill Bailey. I said these words: "Brother Bill, I'm surrendering to the ministry. I believe I've been called to preach." Bro. Bill simply replied, "I've been waiting on you!" He then instructed me to sit on the front pew while he continued the invitation. It was a remarkably emotional experience.

Patsy soon came to the front pew to sit with me. We

hugged and cried together. My daughter, Haley, also joined us there. She asked Patsy: "Momma, did Daddy get saved? Did Daddy get saved?" Now that will bless your heart! Here I was, surrendering my life to preach the Gospel, and my daughter was thinking that I was getting saved! Patsy said, "No, dear, your Daddy is surrendering his life to the ministry."

The night before, Patsy and I had talked, sparingly, about the possibility of my becoming a preacher. I told her that God had really placed me under conviction. I also told her that He might have to burn my barley field (because I just didn't believe that I could ever become a preacher)! One of the main reasons I was struggling was because I had been a deacon. I had seen how difficult being a preacher could be. I didn't want any part of that!

Ironically, it was during a Monday night revival service when I surrendered to preach. Just as it was also following a Monday night football game that I had been brought to my knees in surrender to my Lord Jesus Christ!

More than one person at Round Island Baptist Church had discipled and mentored me—in fact, it was the entire body of Christ. They had given me the opportunities and responsibilities within the church that I needed to help me to grow and mature. It's a proven fact—responsibility helps a person grow, because it automatically forces a person to study and learn. That's why I have always enjoyed taking on a variety of duties and responsibilities that have enabled me, and prompted me, to study. Studying, for me, doesn't come naturally—especially reading! I have to discipline myself to read and study the Bible. It truly requires discipline for me to pray and to get into God's Word.

When I took on those responsibilities, it truly helped me to grow and to become obedient to the leadership of God's Spirit. That's why we Christians need to accept responsibilities. It greatly helps in making us disciples of Jesus Christ.

Looking back on my twelve years at Round Island Baptist Church, I can clearly see now just how God used that precious time to prepare me for what, and where, I am now. Most pastors will complete their seminary training in four years; it took me twelve! But, believe me, I gleaned more in those twelve years than I ever could have in a seminary. Nothing could have prepared me any better!

SEVEN

Family and God's Preparation

When our life's journey is viewed from the rearview mirror, we can look back and trace God's hand as He had presented us with opportunities. When God breathed life into Adam, He created him with a free will. That's what makes man unique among all of God's creatures. God allows us to live our lives as we choose—even if it's in opposition to His will. Someone once said, "Of all of God's creations, man is the only one who can say, 'No' to God."

As a man, God holds me responsible for the care, protection and leadership of my family. Therefore, my choice to gamble was my decision. The consequences for that choice were laid at my feet. But God redeemed me with the precious blood of His Son and my Savior, Jesus Christ! God allowed me to make the choice to sin. In spite of all that I had done, He still loved me and redeemed me.

After thirty-four years of salvation, I have never lost my gratitude for His redemption. God's grace and mercy have restored me, both as a husband and as the leader of my family. God's love has truly set me upon a path that I had honestly never considered possible. His forgiveness has given me the will to live and to carry on. I've never gotten over God's wonderful, amazing grace!

While I was working at Helena Chemical Company, in the summer of 1974, I heard that the Monsanto Chemical Company in Decatur, Alabama, was hiring. I put in an application. I was hired after a friend, Cloyd Pepper, took my application to the right people. At that time, Monsanto was producing a variety of textile fabrics (such as wigs and Astro-Turf). They also produced various chemical compounds. As an aside, Monsanto made the first Astro-Turf that was used in the Astrodome in Houston, Texas.

I began working as a machine operator. Eventually, I was transferred to the polyester division, where I performed multiple jobs.

After I had worked at Monsanto for nine years, production began to decline. Due to a national financial recession, I was eventually moved to another area in the plant. My new job was to supervise seventeen women in the janitorial department. I received absolutely no training for the job! That was quite an experience, to say the least!

Family and God's Preparation

Looking back, I now realize that God was developing my leadership skills. He was preparing me to fulfill His plan for my life.

I was laid off, and eventually let go, from the Monsanto Chemical Company. Our nation was in a severe economic recession, so I had great difficulty finding full-time employment.

In order to supplement my unemployment income, I became a summer league baseball umpire. I umpired for the city and county leagues, as well as high school baseball games. For many months, I worked almost every day as an umpire. I made many friends—and many enemies!

Right before I was laid off, our second daughter, JoDare, was born (April of 1982). I was unemployed, receiving unemployment checks, and umpiring summer league ball games in order to support my family. Haley was almost seven years old; JoDare was an infant; we were all living in our 12 x 65, two-bedroom trailer. We were even receiving food stamps for a couple of months![13]

It was really tough, financially, for our family during this time. At times, I would feel so confused and so desperate. But God was growing my faith and my ability to trust in Him.

On one occasion, we were almost out of money. A check

---

[13] I made Patsy go get the food stamps because I had too much pride. Pride was, by the way, a big part of my problem. Everything was all about me!

for $75 arrived in the mailbox from Monsanto. Apparently, there had been a chemical spill a few months earlier near the parking lot where I had been assigned to park. The chemical had scattered everywhere, covering several vehicles. Monsanto sent money to all of the individuals that had parked in those lots as compensation for any potential damages.[14]

Patsy had revealed to me earlier that same day that we didn't have much food. We both just stared at each other, recognizing that the money had truly been a providential blessing from God!

Even though we were living in difficult financial circumstances, our faith never faltered. We went to church every time that the doors were open! We both knew that God had saved us. We truly desired to be faithful to our Lord. Our faith has carried us through the good times, as well as some very difficult times.

I eventually found a job at Tennessee Valley Wholesales in Athens, Alabama, where they sold plumbing and electrical supplies. I was hired to work at the sales counter. That is where I met the wife of Steelcase's Human Resources (HR) manager, Leon Simmons. This would become another turning point in my life.

Mrs. Simmons (Joan) came into the store, one day, to buy some lamp fixtures. I knew that she was the HR

---

[14] I did not notice any damage to my car at the time, but everyone that had possibly been affected received a payment.

Family and God's Preparation

manager's wife, so I quickly asked if I could help her. I had truly been praying that I would have an opportunity to talk with her about a job at Steelcase! I remember that I told her that I would get her anything she needed—she would just need to let me know!

I subsequently asked her to put in a good word for me with her husband, since he was doing all of the hiring at Steelcase. Unbelievably, when she went home, she told Mr. Simmons that he needed to hire me—she felt that I had a great personality.

Leon Simmons called me at my job the next day. He invited me to come *to his house* for an interview! At the conclusion of the interview, he told me to report to Steelcase on the following Monday morning for a physical examination. I arrived on Monday, passed the physical exam, and began my new career with Steelcase. I was placed into an assembly area, forming and assembling sheet metal into a variety of office furniture items. Wow! God is truly amazing!

After a few years working in the assembly area, I was promoted to the position of supervisor on the night shift. One year later, I was offered—and accepted—the opportunity to begin training to become a mechanical engineer. The in-house program was primarily on-the-job training. Soon afterwards, I had a new job title: Mechanical Engineer. Life was definitely looking up!

Now free from the addiction of gambling, I was able to truly enjoy my life. The four of us were growing into a strong, loving family. One of our favorite pastimes was playing softball. That's not surprising, since I grew up playing baseball. I have always loved the game.

Haley and JoDare both received their passion for softball from me, their Daddy! They had started playing softball when they were each about five years old.

Patsy had wanted them, especially JoDare, to be more feminine. She was hoping that JoDare would have been less tomboyish than her sister, Haley. But their Dad, wanting them to play softball, won the day.

Haley, born seven years before JoDare, definitely got the brunt of the pressure from her Dad. I had wanted her to become a chip off the old block! She was the "boy" I had always desired! I wanted Haley to be tough, so I was a very strict disciplinarian with her.

I was Haley's coach during summer league fast-pitch softball. As a coach's daughter, Haley had it really tough—I demanded perfection. I was living out my baseball dreams through my daughter. Like hosts of other parents are guilty of doing, I think I was caught up in the expectations of my child becoming the best athlete. And, honestly, Haley rose to the occasion. She excelled to become one of the best players on her team! During her senior year, she would

Family and God's Preparation

become one of only two players on her high school team to make All State.

Next it was JoDare's turn! But, by this time, I had grown a little wiser. I had matured somewhat. I didn't press her as much as I had pressed Haley. Also, I discovered that JoDare did not respond to being pressured in the same way that Haley had. She was more sensitive and tenderhearted. She would either pout or cry when I looked sternly at her. Her sister, Haley, had learned to just tune me out!

As a Dad, I could not have been more proud of both of my daughters. Thank God that I eventually came to the realization that my daughters were not playing the game for me! These would become precious years for our family. Parenthetically, God continues to bless our family through softball—with our grandchildren.

Well, life in our family was about to take a major turn. My time at Steelcase was coming to an end; consequently, our family life was about to be dramatically transformed. I had begun substituting for vacationing pastors in a couple of churches.

One day, during work at Steelcase, a friend named Todd Brown asked me a question that would ultimately change my life. He asked me to preach at his little church—Lindsay Lane. Little did either of us know that this would become the beginning of a total God-thing! It would change my family members' lives in ways that we had never anticipated.

I had preached there only twice when the members of Lindsay Lane asked me to become their pastor. So, in April of 1992, I became the bivocational pastor of Lindsay Lane Baptist Church! At that time, the church had only thirty-two members.

During my last two years at Steelcase, I was working full-time at the plant, serving as the bivocational pastor at Lindsay Lane, and attending Heritage Bible College in Huntsville. My plate was becoming more than full, but I was *finally* doing what God called me to do! My life as a pastor was truly a work-in-progress!

After two years as a bivocational pastor, the church had grown to the point where I could no longer simultaneously serve both Steelcase and Lindsay Lane. The money was at Steelcase, but my heart was at Lindsay Lane! In August 1994, the plant manager at Steelcase called me into his office. He said, "Dusty, I have heard that you're leaving us to pastor a small church here in Athens. I know how much your salary is here; I don't understand how you're going to make it financially."

I just told him, "Jim, I don't really know, either. All I know is that God has called me to preach. The church is offering me a salary, and I'll have my severance pay from Steelcase. I'm going to live on that money until January, when the church will be able to bring me on as their full-time pastor." I also remember that I told Jim that, while sitting in my office at Steelcase, staring at all of the charts and graphs, my heart was really at Lindsay Lane.

I resigned from Steelcase in September of 1994 so that I could work full-time at Lindsay Lane. The church couldn't pay me a full-time salary until January 1995. It was kind of scary! At first, Patsy was very nervous. But we both knew that God would provide. We had a peace about the situation, because we knew the church was growing.

I was now the full-time pastor of the church. My schedule was becoming so demanding that I considered dropping out of Bible College. I am so thankful, however, that I stuck with it and completed my studies!

Those first years were difficult not only for me, but also for my entire family. Patsy and the girls endured my absence with grace and mercy. It would be many years later, but I finally realized that my priorities in life should be God, then family, and then the church. And in that order! God's hand was upon me and my family during those years. Patsy had super strength; she became my rock.

The decision to leave Steelcase and become the Pastor of Lindsay Lane was a lot easier than our previous decision to move our family's membership to Lindsay Lane from Round Island in 1992. Haley, JoDare, and even Patsy cried during the transition. But they knew that God had called us to serve at Lindsay Lane. The girls would ask if they could go to Sunday school at Round Island, because they didn't know anyone at Lindsay Lane. There were only two teenagers at Lindsay Lane in the early days, and one of them was Haley. JoDare was about to turn ten years old—she didn't know anyone, either. After a couple of weeks, I told my family that God had called all of us as a family—not just me. Patsy and I encouraged Haley to help grow the Lindsay Lane youth group by inviting her friends to church. This was difficult for her, as she had never been on a youth trip or any church activities outside of those at Round Island. I challenged her to be a leader, and to help us develop a youth group at Lindsay Lane. God was at work. He was growing me personally, our children, and His church!

In December of 1992, Haley presented us with a new challenge. At the age of seventeen, she announced to us that she and her boyfriend, Chuck Robinson, were engaged! Chuck had given her an engagement ring for Christmas. Patsy and I were totally shocked! We refused to accept this—she was too young and was not ready for marriage. Additionally, Chuck had not asked us for permission to marry our daughter! We felt this was very disrespectful and that Chuck, at that time, was demonstrating a very controlling personality. Haley and Chuck were always together. They

Family and God's Preparation

rarely spent time with our family. Chuck seemed to want Haley all to himself.

Haley was caught in the middle. Her softball coach wanted her to play ball, Chuck wanted her to be with him, and Patsy and I wanted her to be our full-time daughter! We didn't want her to marry Chuck—we didn't think the time (or the person) was right. Patsy was having such a hard time with Haley getting married at such a young age that their relationship suffered as a result. Resentment soon followed on both of their parts.

Then, one day, I was listening to James Dobson on the radio. He was telling the story of his children growing up. God used that message to settled things for me. I went home and told Patsy that there was nothing we could do about Haley's and Chuck's relationship, but pray. They were going to get married—regardless of our desires.

God gave me peace about the two of them getting married. He told me that, even though she was only eighteen years old, she was old enough to go to college at John C. Calhoun and, therefore, she was old enough to make this other decision. Patsy and I prayed through that situation. We were not willing to lose our relationship with Haley, so we resolved to accept her decision to marry. So, on February 5, 1994, Haley and Chuck Robinson became the very first couple to be married at Lindsay Lane Baptist

Church! Guess who married them?

Prior to this event, Chuck and I had talked about his salvation. He had realized that he was lost. Not long after their wedding, Chuck gave his life to Jesus. He was able to start a brand-new life with Christ and with a new wife. It was my great joy and honor to baptize Chuck, not only as my son-in-law but also as my brother in Christ!

Although he had been saved and baptized, it would still take time for our relationship to grow into what it needed to be—and into what it is today. In those early days, Chuck was a bit standoffish with us—especially with me. I soon discovered that it was partly due to the fact that he was afraid of me.

Years later, Chuck finally told me about it. One of Chuck's most vivid memories was the night on which I took him bass fishing on the Elk River. It was just the two of us. He had been aware of the friction between us (but I was just trying to be friendly). When we were almost to the lake, I asked him to retrieve something from the car's glove compartment. When he opened the glove compartment, he saw the pistol I always kept there. He was suddenly terrified—he thought I intended to shoot him! Now every time he tells that story, we all have a good laugh. It is amazing how God is able to change things!

Our relationship with Chuck really blossomed two hours

after our second grandson was born. Chuck is an emotional guy. That day in February 1997, Patsy and I were in the hospital room with Chuck, Haley, and baby Luke. We watched Chuck as he held his son. He began to shed tears of joy.

He shared his heart with us in that hospital room. He told us, "When I was fifteen years old, I prayed to God. I told Him that all I ever wanted was to be part of a Christian family." Needless to say, Chuck immediately stole our hearts! From that point on, our love for him has continued to grow. It is amazing how God works all things for good for those who love the Lord![15]

---

[15] Romans 8:28.

EIGHT

Called Out by God

God calls men, such as the Apostle Paul, into the ministry. When you read the accounts of God's calling upon the lives of the prophets Jeremiah and Isaiah, you can get a sense of how God places His anointing upon His chosen men.

Moses is a good example of how someone is called, or specifically chosen, by God. God led Moses to the top of Mount Sinai, where He sanctified and appointed him for the specific task of leading the Israelites out of Egypt. God anointed Moses to become their leader. He equipped him to make crucial leadership decisions and to serve as a judge over the people.

Eventually, however, God led Moses' father-in-law, Jethro, to inform Moses that he couldn't continue doing everything by himself. Jethro advised Moses to choose other leaders to share the responsibilities for a designated number of people. Although Moses had delegated a few of his responsibilities, he remained the leader of the people.

Near Moses' death, God chose Joshua to become Moses' successor. Joshua would, therefore, assume the role as leader of all of the Israelites that came out of Egypt.

As a God-anointed and sanctified leader, I believe that God speaks directly to me. He has chosen me and called me for His specific service. That doesn't mean that God will not speak to, and through, others. But it *does* mean that God places His hand and His Spirit of authority upon His "called out" leader. I personally believe that I'm held accountable to God for how I lead His church at Lindsay Lane. If I were to say something like, "Well, I'll just let the deacons make the decisions," I don't believe God would hold the deacons accountable for the major decisions they would make on behalf of the church. But I do believe that He would hold me, as the senior pastor, accountable. God would come looking for *me*!

This happened in the Garden of Eden. God didn't look for Eve, even though she was the first to eat the fruit—God came looking for Adam. God singled Adam out, because God had placed Adam in authority. Adam, therefore, was accountable to God for whatever happened in the Garden.

The concept of the "headship role" is clearly taught in the Bible.[16] God has expanded this concept to extend to

---

[16] Ephesians 5:23.

His authoritative plan for His chosen man and the church. He does not call and sanctify the senior pastor to rule as a dictator over the members of the church but, rather, to lead them. The senior pastor must, therefore, lead the congregation in the way that God is leading him. I, therefore, as the senior pastor and the man that God has chosen to lead His church, must cast the vision for the church in concert with the way in which God's Spirit is leading me. I can't lead by my own intuition, or in my own wisdom. I need the support of my staff, the deacon body, and the support of the congregation. But, at the end of the day, I am ultimately responsible for leading Lindsay Lane.

This leadership responsibility is described in Hebrews 13:17:

> *Obey those who rule over you, and be submissive, for they watch out for your souls, as **those who must give account** [emphasis mine]. Let them do so with joy and not with grief, for that would be unprofitable for you.*

The senior pastor's calling and role are twofold: to be the shepherd and the overseer of the church. The Apostle Peter admonishes us:[17]

> *The elders who are among you I exhort, I who am a fellow elder and a witness of the sufferings of Christ, and also a partaker of the glory that will be revealed. Shepherd the flock*

---
[17] 1 Peter 5:1-3.

> *of God which is among you, serving as overseers, not by compulsion but willingly, not for dishonest gain but eagerly; nor as being lords over those entrusted to you, but being examples to the flock.*

The writer of Hebrews also lends this specific and pointed instruction: *"Remember those who rule over you, who have spoken the word of God to you, whose faith follow, considering the outcome of their conduct."*[18]

Scripture is very clear about the fact that the *"pastor"* or the *"shepherd"* must be the leader of the church. The congregation is to pray for, as well as follow, their leader. Many churches have experienced enormous problems, because they have been unwilling to follow this fundamental and biblical instruction relating to God's order for leadership in the church!

At Lindsay Lane, our senior ministerial staff members serve in the dual capacity of Elders and Pastors. But God called me to be the *senior* Pastor and Elder. The pastor and senior staff members are called to jointly be the *"overseers"* of the church.

God has called me to Lindsay Lane to be a godly leader, and not just to be the preacher. The members of Lindsay Lane greatly needed a leader to shepherd them. They needed someone to lead them, and to cast God's vision for His

---

[18] Hebrews 13:7.

church before them. They needed a pastor to lead them, and to proclaim, "This is how I'm going to lead you, and how I will seek God's will for this church."

I believe God has blessed the people of Lindsay Lane over the years for their obedience in following the directives of His Word. At the end of the day, as senior pastor, I have personally assumed all of the responsibility for serving and leading His church.

All senior pastors will eventually be challenged in their capacity as leaders! That's why I believe it's essential for me to know that God has called me. I also need to follow the leadership of His Holy Spirit in my life and service.

Fear can paralyze a pastor. He must never allow himself to become constantly worried about either making a wrong decision, or having his leadership challenged by certain members or groups within the church.

Leadership can be difficult at times. It's like a coach who's facing fourth down and inches. He's the coach and the leader. He must make a crucial decision. If he is constantly thinking about what the fans will think, then he is not leading! Rather, he is yielding his leadership role to others, instead of performing the job that he has been hired to do: "lead the team" as the head coach!

Whether you have been called to be a coach or a pastor, you must be willing to accept the consequences of your decisions. But I also believe that, if the Senior Pastor is going to have to *take* the shots, then he must also have the authority to *call* the shots! And, believe me, if he doesn't make those critical calls, others will try to make them for him! In the words of Allan Taylor, Minister of Education at the First Baptist Church of Woodstock, GA, "It's easy to make a call when you're sitting in the stands with a hotdog in your hand!"

A pastor will always need others to help him. He must be willing delegate some of the decision-making. That's why God told Moses, through Jethro, to seek out men to become members of his staff! The pastor needs others to come alongside of him to support him and to help him make crucial decisions.

But, at the end of the day, the final call will rest squarely upon the pastor as the leader. The leader has been called and hired to make decisions. That is exactly what he, as a good leader, must do.

In my twenty-two years as pastor of Lindsay Lane, I've had to make many decisions. The most recent decision was to erect a Children's Building to accommodate our church's continued growth. Additionally, I also knew we would eventually need space to fulfill our vision for a Christian Academy. I earnestly sought God's will regarding this decision.

If I sincerely believe that I am doing what God is leading me to do, then I will have confidence. If I don't have that confidence, then I must wait upon God before making the decision!

I had to make my first major decision as pastor of Lindsay Lane in 1993. I led the church to build a fellowship hall and an education wing. At the time, we were a small congregation without any money. But the members of the congregation caught the vision, and they supported it. The reward I personally received was the joy of watching our people and the church as they were growing!

Looking back over my tenure at Lindsay Lane, the hardest decision I have ever had to make (with regards to building construction) was constructing the new Children's Building. It would be a 42,000 square foot, state of the art building! We had already built a new sanctuary in 2002. We had, therefore, already accumulated some major debt. But we were out of space and needed more room for our children.

God kept sending us so many children that we were holding AWANA classes in hallways and in closets. I continuously heard teachers asking, "What should we do? We don't have any room?"

So, naturally, I began to seriously seek the Lord in prayer. I said, "Lord if you're going to keep sending children, then You will need to provide the space." I earnestly believe that the Lord answered me when He led me to build the Children's Building!

There was opposition, of course, and understandably so. We had a large debt to consider. But I truly believed we were building this new Children's Building for the children that God was sending, and would continue to send, to us. We simply needed more space for them than what we currently had. That's where I think some churches make their biggest mistake: they try to build for what they already have, rather than seeking God for the number of people that He's leading them to reach.

I certainly believe it's wise to do your homework. You should also know the facts, as much as possible, so that you can answer any questions your people may have. But a major investment of time in prayer and thought into your decision-making will help increase your confidence that God is leading the effort.

Before we built the Children's Building, I asked a couple of my ministerial staff members, Bradley Griggs and Sonny Schofield, to evaluate several items: our growth charts from previous years, our existing debt, the demographics of the area, and where we, as a church, expected to be in our attendance over the next three to five years. I wanted to know the numbers so that I could make an informed decision.

It was a difficult decision, but it was the right decision.

By God's grace, we have grown numerically, and we have filled the large building with a host of God's children! To God be the glory!

Over these past twenty-two years God has, on many occasions, confirmed the decisions I've had to make. God has graciously helped me as I have taken some small steps as a leader; He has grown me personally as I have also taken several more significant steps.

Let me share just one example of just how God guides us in working through difficult issues. I had two very close friends, who were also serving as two of my deacons. In 1993, they had been opposed to building what would become the Fellowship Hall and education wings of the church. As highly successful businessmen, they thought that the church couldn't afford such a large financial undertaking. They said, "It just doesn't work on paper." And, in their defense, it probably didn't. But the church must operate by faith, especially when facing crucial decisions!

So I waited a couple of months. I prayed, and earnestly sought, God's will and direction. And then I brought the need to build before the members of the congregation for a second time. This time, it was supported. We went forward by faith. Because of our continued growth, the debt was quickly paid!

About six months after we had moved into the new

building, those same two deacons who that previously opposed the building project came to me. They gave me their votes of confidence. They were now in full support of the expansion! They didn't admit that I had been right but, rather, that God had been leading me to do it. And now they could also understand and see it.

I recall hearing my mentor Johnny Hunt once proclaim, *"If you don't see it before you see it, you'll never see it!"* That phrase expresses the need for both faith and vision!

My faith is no more special than anyone else's to God. But, since God has called me to be the shepherd (pastor) and, therefore, the leader of the church, He will usually speak first to me. I will, in turn, reveal God's will to the rest of His people.

Sometimes, in the quietness of the night, I will be unable to sleep. I will wonder if I've truly understood God's will. That's when I go back to His Word for reassurance of His guidance and for confidence. When God tells us, "You will seek Me and find Me when you seek Me with all your heart,"[19] He isn't speaking in riddles so that He can trip me up! He is speaking the truth. He is saying exactly what He means. I believe that God desires His servant to lead out in faith. He wants to build up our confidence and our faith in Him.

For example, God told Abraham to go up on the

---

[19] Deuteronomy 4:29.

Called Out by God

mountain. He commanded Abraham to sacrifice his son, Isaac. Abraham didn't really receive an explanation; he just did what God had instructed him to do. When Abraham obeyed, the Bible says, "It was accounted to him as righteousness."[20]

I'm sure Abraham learned obedience in the big things, because he had seen the faithfulness of God in his obedience in the little things. That's why the Bible exhorts us, "Without faith, it is impossible to please God."[21]

I'm sure the enemy has often planted seeds of doubt in my mind. He has caused me to ask the question, "How are we going to get that much money?" That's when I follow Jesus' pattern of answering the temptations of the devil—with God's Word.

I've found that God always blesses two things: His Word and obedience to His Word! I try to keep in mind that, when it comes to financial issues, we're dealing with people's lives and livelihoods. I'm constantly challenging them to give their hard earned money in support of the ministry of God's church. I don't care how good a leader you are; if people don't have confidence in God's faithfulness to keep the promises in His Word, they will not give. I certainly don't want people to place their faith in me. I want them to believe in, and trust, God! As Pastor, I've already seen what the church needs. I know what God has previously done in

---

[20] Galatians 3:6. [21] Hebrews 11:6.

this church. I now must lead our people to see the vision that God has placed before us. Taking on a major project involves much more than buildings and mortgages—it also helps breed and build faith in the lives of people!

Lindsay Lane caught the vision that God had given me years ago—to develop a congregation that resembles heaven. That is, believers of multiple races and cultures coming together to worship God, and to exalt His Son Jesus Christ.

Our church is quickly becoming a multicultural church. Our vision statement says that Lindsay Lane is a church for all people! I'm very excited that our people have caught the vision of accepting people for whom they are in Christ!

Our "Hungry for Him" Street Ministry has brought several homeless people to our church. The members of our congregation have welcomed, encouraged, and supported these homeless people in many ways. For example, when one homeless couple was married in our church, someone baked the wedding cake; others chipped in and financed the entire wedding—they even paid for the honeymoon!

A church that desires to grow must realize that growth will bring many changes. It will also require a lot of hard work! For a very long time (until we built our new building), I preached during two Sunday morning worship service. The number of people in attendance, coupled with the limited size of our facilities, had required us to meet during two separate Sunday school times for years! Due to our growth, and the fact that we are now serving many more families, we've added more staff members and deacons. Believe me, it has nothing to do either with a desire for prosperity or for becoming the "largest" congregation in town—it's about *intentional evangelism*: serving people to make Christ known to the nations.

If you're committed to God and to growing His kingdom, you'll soon develop a "whatever it takes" mentality—regardless of the cost. It all comes down to discipline, commitment, and passion for God's Word and His kingdom's work. We're all called to reach the world, including all manners of people. If we need to build another building, go to three or more services, or make ourselves more available, those of us at Lindsay Lane are willing to do "whatever it takes." Our people have caught that type of vision!

I think one of the reasons that Lindsay Lane has been so successful is that we have developed a group of staff members and a leadership team that are sold out and committed to what God has called us to do. We are leading by example!

Homer Lindsay, Jr.[22] once told a group of ministers, "It will take about six years before you are actually accepted as the pastor of the church." People will not follow you until they have learned to trust your heart. They will need the assurance that you're not just passing through, looking for the

---

[22] Former pastor of First Baptist Church of Jacksonville, FL

"greener pastures" of a bigger church. Once they feel they truly know you are their pastor and leader and that you're the real deal, committed for the long haul—then, and only then, will the members of the congregation embrace and faithfully support you as their pastor.

NINE

Sharing My Faith

Witnessing is something that God has commanded us to do. The Bible says, "Go therefore and make disciples of all the nations."[23] The Greek text literally says, "As you are going." So, *as we go* about our everyday lives, we are to share our faith—become "witnesses." We can witness verbally. We can also witness by living our lives in such a way that we demonstrate to others what Christ has done, and is doing, for us through His Gospel. Even though God has commanded us to go and to share the Gospel, we will do it simply because it is who we are in Christ!

Other people will truly know when our lives are reflecting Jesus Christ. When people ask what has changed us, we're given the opportunity to share our faith. An eyewitness in a courtroom gives testimony to what he or she has seen firsthand. As Christians, we give testimony to what Christ

---

[23] Matthew 28:19.

has done in changing our lives. There are many methods we can use in sharing our faith: following the "Romans Road,"[24] explaining the meanings of various scriptures (such as John 3:16), or using a Gospel tract.

As soon as I was saved, God led me to share what Christ had done for me with others. But I needed to learn how to do that. My training would begin in Sunday school at Round Island.

I've witnessed to many people during my lifetime. I continue to do so whenever God places an opportunity before me.

I would like to mention four special men—men that have become my close friends, and with whom I have had the privilege of sharing the message of Jesus Christ. They are Mike Adams, Stan Holt, Randy Brown, and Eddy McLemore.

Mike Adams

The first time I witnessed intentionally was to the husband of a lady named Tammy Adams, a member of my Sunday school class at Round Island. I had noticed that Tammy's husband was never with her when she came to church.

One Sunday, I asked Tammy about her husband. She told me, "He doesn't go to church." I asked her if I could visit with him at their home. She said that would be great.

---

[24] Romans 3:23, 6:23, 5:8, 10:9, 10:10, and 10:13.

So she and I set a time for me to visit with him.

A few days later my pastor, Bill Bailey, and I visited together with Mike. Before our visit Tammy had told Mike that we were coming to visit. And she also told him the reason why.

Mike was (and still is) a very friendly person, and very easy to talk to. I wanted to get to know him better before we talked with him about Christ. So I began my conversation with Mike by talking about his construction business. We then talked about another one of his interests—Alabama football.[25] Later, I told Mike that, since Tammy was a member of my Sunday school class, Bro. Bill and I had come for the dual purposes of meeting him and inviting him to church.

After I had invited him to Sunday school, Mike said, "I might do that. I'll think about it." He told us that, when he was a child, he did go to church. But he was not currently living his life as a Christian. As we were leaving, we told Mike that we hoped that he would respond to our invitation by coming to church with Tammy.

Mike *did* respond to our visit. He came to Round Island the next Sunday and also attended Sunday school with Tammy. Not long after that initial visit, Mike joined me on

---

[25] It's important to develop a personal relationship with someone before attempting to share Jesus with them. Finding commonalities you have with someone is crucial in the witnessing process. If you see a fish mounted on the wall, you will know that person is a fisherman.

a Wednesday night to visit another family and invite them to Round Island.

Mike continued to attend church for about four weeks. I sat with him during the service. Prior to that Sunday, Mike and I had often talked about our growth in the Lord, and how we were continuously seeking to know Him. During the altar call, I asked him, "Mike, do you want to go up? If you want to go up and receive Jesus, I'll go with you. I'll be there for you and I'll help you."

He squeezed my hand as he said, "I don't know. I don't know." He just stood there, tightly squeezing my hand with his powerful grip.

I said, "Mike, I'll go with you. Are you ready?"

He made his commitment with one simple word: "Alright."

Together, we walked the aisle. Mike told our pastor, Bill Bailey, that he had come for the purpose of receiving Christ. I then took Mike into a private room and shared Christ with him. I explained how he, too, could become a Christian. That morning, Mike prayed the "Sinner's Prayer."[26] He invited Jesus Christ into his heart and life!

Mike continued to attend church in the weeks and months that followed. His life had been thoroughly changed.

---

[26] Mike admitted that he had a time in his life when he had disobeyed God. He also recognized the fact that his sins had separated him from God. He wanted to begin a relationship with God, so he asked Him to forgive him for his sins, to come into his life, and to give him eternal life through Jesus Christ.

In fact, Mike became a soul winner! Mike was (and still is) very outgoing; he was never shy! He has always been one of those guys who is not afraid to share his faith.

Mike became a very faithful member of our Sunday school class. As our friendship grew, Mike realized that my first visit with him had not been simply an attempt to get him to buy into something. Rather, he learned that I had been concerned about him, and that I now considered him as a friend. Our relationship grew to the point at which Patsy and I began to take our vacations with Mike and Tammy.

Meeting Mike, and walking the aisle with him, was based upon building, and then continuing, a relationship with him. Both witnessing and discipleship are all about relationships. Once people get to know you, and they see your heart, they will begin to realize that you're not just trying to sell them something. They will begin to view you, not as a Sunday school teacher or a pastor but as a friend. Before surrendering their lives to Christ, their primary relationships have been with lost people; they need to learn that they can also have friendships with Christians.

One of the barriers you will have to break down is the perception that lost people have about Christians being "holier than thou." If you can do that, a lost person will be more likely to listen to you.

Nine months after I surrendered to preach, I became

Lindsay Lane's pastor. Mike and Tammy joined our small, but growing, church. They came to Lindsay Lane because they wanted to help me, and they wanted to help grow our small church.

For the purpose of this book, I asked Mike to describe his impression of my first visit, and the early days of our friendship. This is what he recalled:

> *I was saved at a revival that Aubrey Rose preached. You and I went out for visitation that Saturday morning. I was witnessing to people and was as lost as a ball in high weeds. During the revival, I went all week holding onto the pew. You were in the choir every night where I could see you, but that Wednesday, the last night of the revival, I didn't see you in the choir. I finally saw you sitting right in front of me! At the end of the service, I was crying and holding on to the pew as tight as I could. You grabbed my hand and said, "I'll go with you." (Thank you for not going to the choir that night!) When we got to the altar, you and Brother Bill prayed with me. The devil was about to lose a good worker!*

He continued,

> *When you and Brother Bill came to visit me for the first time, I came to the door with a beer in my hand. I thought, to myself, "Y'all are not going to change me." Thank God that I was wrong*

Mike has become a very faithful Christian. Over the years, he has continued to support both our church and me personally. He does not do anything for applause or recognition. Mike is simply a faithful Christian who loves the Lord, and witnesses without fear. Lindsay Lane is blessed to have him as an active church member!

Mike's life has been changed, and I have gained a very special, close friend. To this day, our friendship is very strong. Mike still attends Lindsay Lane, where he is a witnessing machine!

Stan Holt

In the next chapter, you will read about two drinking buddies that walked the aisle to accept Christ.[27] One of them was Bill Holt, Stan's father. Stan and I had known each other during our high school days. He had attended Athens High School; I went to Tanner High. We met while playing in a flag football league.

As our friendship grew, we started going to a place called "Dugger's" in Tennessee to drink. Stan and I also gambled on football games through a local bookie, and we often watched football games together. We even went one time to Tuscaloosa to watch Alabama play LSU.

Patsy and I remained friends with Stan and his wife, Lynn, after I was saved in 1979. We frequently ate at each

---

[27] See Chapter Ten: The Lindsay Lane Vision

other's houses. We just hung out together, as friends often do.

Sadly, Stan and Lynn eventually divorced. After that, Stan and I began to spend more time together. We would play softball, or just hang out at his house. I continued to talk to Stan about his need for Christ coming into his life, but he wasn't ready.

Stan began to party heavily and chase women. Even so, because we were good friends, we continued to stay in touch. He would often call me just to talk, or to ask if I had seen Alabama play that week. We continued to play softball together and stayed in close contact.

Stan was not a bad guy. He just liked to have a good time.

I knew Stan was constantly watching my life. And so, one night in 1992 (after I had surrendered to preach), he asked if I would come over to his house and talk with him. By this time, since we were not seeing each other on a regular basis, our friendship had begun to dwindle. He'd been dating a woman for more than a year, but she had just walked out on him. When I arrived, I could tell he was very upset.

Stan told me, "I don't know what I'm going to do with my life."

I said to him, "Stan, what you need is the Lord Jesus in your life. I've been trying to talk to you about Him for a long time now!"

He replied, "I don't know how! What do I need to do?"

Stan was finally broken! I told him what he needed was to accept Christ as his personal Savior, and then follow-through with believers' baptism. And so he did. He came to church and walked down the aisle. I had the privilege of baptizing him in the baptistery of our original sanctuary.

By this time his dad had died, so he did not have the opportunity of seeing his son saved and baptized. However, Stan's mother, Louise, began attending Lindsay Lane with him.

After a few months, however, Stan started fading away from the church. We were still playing softball together, so I talked to him about coming back to church. He would usually tell me that he'd be there the next Sunday—but he never came. He began associating with the same types of friends he had before he was saved. I knew he was headed for trouble!

I kept talking to Stan about the Lord. He was traveling to Tunica, Mississippi, to gamble at the casinos. The manager of one of the casinos eventually gave him a complimentary suite. Stan began taking his friends with him, putting them up for the night in his suite, and gambling with them at the casino.

Throughout all of this, he still carried a Bible verse on a

card that he kept it in his wallet. I don't remember the verse. But I will always remember that, when he gave me one of the cards, he asked me to come with him for a weekend at the casino. Stan told me that he wasn't gambling; he was just bringing some friends with him to have a good time.

He frequently asked Patsy and me to join him at the casino as his guests. I told him, "Stan, I can't go there. I don't want to go there and be tempted. I appreciate the offer, but I just don't live that lifestyle anymore." Stan kept insisting that all he was doing was having a good time at Tunica; everything was okay.

Stan was a bodybuilder and, therefore, very muscular. He worked out regularly, competed in bodybuilding events, and even won the Mr. Alabama competition. Women were physically attracted to Stan, and he loved it. Stan was a handsome and well-built man but, in my opinion, he was hung-up on himself. He liked the fact that women were attracted to him.

A while after I had declined his invitation to go with him to Tunica, I could tell that something was bothering him. One day I asked him, "Stan, are you gambling again? Are you in trouble?" He said, "No, there's just some things going on with a girlfriend again."

One Friday night, he called to tell me he was at a rehab center for gambling, anxiety, and depression. His cousin,

Phil, had driven him to the facility. He was supposed to be there for the entire weekend. The next day, Saturday, he called Phil again. He told Phil that he didn't want to stay at the facility any longer. Phil went to the facility, picked up Stan, and then drove him home.

When Stan arrived home, he told his Mom that he was going into his room for a little bit. His Mom asked him to come into the living room to talk to her. He said, "No," and then he walked into his room. He retrieved his gun from a drawer, and shot himself!

As soon as I heard the news, I wept. When I arrived at the house, his body was still in the bedroom and his mother was grieving. She had heard the shot, and had known what had happened. I stayed until his body was removed to comfort the family. It was a horrible situation, one that I will never be able to forget.

As Stan's pastor, I preached his funeral. His bodybuilding friends carried him to his grave. That day, I preached the Gospel of Jesus Christ! To this day, I believe Stan was a Christian—that he had received Jesus Christ as his Savior.

I shared Stan's testimony at the funeral. I told how I was with him when he accepted Christ. I spoke about his walking the aisle, accepting Christ, and his baptism. I also talked about how he had attended church for a few months, but how he had slowly returned to his old lifestyle.

Stan, I believe, was trying to keep one foot in the world and the other in the church. When that happens, life is miserable. He thought he was having a good time but, evidently, he really wasn't. I think one reason for his final difficulties was due to the fact that he was a Christian who was doing things that he wasn't supposed to do.

Some people don't have a church background or get involved in a church. They will remain confused about life. Stan was one of those people. He didn't know many people in the church, and so he didn't spend much time with other Christians. Addressing the Christians in the audience, I said, "That's why it is so imperative that we build good relationships and make friends within the church."

It really hurt me when Stan killed himself. I was one of his best friends, but I had failed to disciple him. Even so, I have peace about it now. I do believe he is in heaven. Though he struggled outwardly, I saw his life change somewhat inwardly. I truly believe that he did give his life to Christ, and that he did so sincerely. Unfortunately, Stan drifted from following Christ by allowing his flesh to follow the world.

Randy Brown

Patsy and I were living on the West side of Athens, Alabama, in 1996. As a result, every day I had a long drive to the church. We decided to move closer to the church, so we started looking at lots where we could build our new house.

My cousin, Steve Smith, owned a corner lot in the new Forest Hills subdivision. He told me that he had decided not to build on the lot, and that he wanted to sell it. I took Patsy to see the lot, and she really liked it. I didn't know it at the time, but she later returned to the lot to pray over it. She asked God if this was where He wanted us to live.

On her birthday in October of 1996, I gave her a card on which I had written, "I love you and here's your gift. I bought the lot." I had secretly purchased the lot without her knowing about it!

We worked together on getting the land ready for us to build our new house. Our new home would become the fifth house built in the new subdivision. Construction of our house began in November of 1996; we moved into it in January of 1997.

Randy and Jennifer Brown had already started building their new house on the lot beside ours. Randy, a landscape architect, was busy finishing the work on his irrigation system. He had already started working on his new pond and waterfall.

Randy later told me that, when he heard a preacher, was moving in next door, his heart dropped. He immediately placed his waterfall and pond projects on hold, so that he could begin planting an eight-foot evergreen hedge. He called it "the preacher hedge."

While our new house was being built, Patsy and I frequently visited it to check on the progress. We also made landscaping plans for our new lot.

One day, when I was at the lot, Randy was outside working. I went over to introduce myself to him. He said, "Yeah, I heard you were a preacher." I said, "Yes, I'm the pastor at Lindsay Lane." I didn't say anything else at the time, but I did begin to watch him. Randy usually returned home each day about 2:30 in the afternoon to start working in his yard.

I knew Randy was a fisherman, because he had a boat and I often saw him leave with it. I also like to fish so I started talking with him about fishing. I would also talk with him about how I could improve my yard. As you may have guessed, I was intentionally building a relationship with Randy based upon his interests in landscaping and fishing.

As we became friends, Randy began to let down his guard. He began to see me as just a regular guy, not as "the preacher next door."

One day, I decided it was time to talk to him about church. I asked him, "Randy, why don't you come to church with us, and just kick the tires?"

He said, "Well, I go to First Baptist. My wife and I were

married there, and she works in the nursery."

However, he seldom attended First Baptist. When he did, it was only on special occasions.

I asked Randy:

> *Why don't you come to Lindsay Lane this Sunday? I'm preaching a message on fishing. We have the Carpenters for Christ coming, and as I said, I'm speaking on fishing.*

Reluctantly, and without enthusiasm, he said, "Alright, I'll try to come."

The next Sunday, it looked like it was going to rain. Randy decided that he wouldn't be able to work in his yard or go fishing.

I knew that I might just see him in church that morning. Well, he *did* come. He slipped into a pew in the back of the sanctuary. I began talking about fishing, and how the devil will use his lures to deceive and to hook people.

The service was packed. In addition to our regular folks, the Carpenters for Christ were there. They had been in town the previous week building our new sanctuary.

Randy listened to the message, but he didn't say anything about it the next week as we were talking in the yard. He did, however, come back to the church, week after week. If you ask him now, he'll tell you it was, "To hear what the preacher was going to say about my life."

It wasn't too long after he had started to attend regularly that we had a revival at Lindsay Lane. Murray Wilton was the preacher.[28] One night during the revival, Randy accepted Christ as his Savior. Murray had led the congregation in a "Sinner's Prayer,"[29] and asked those in the congregation that had prayed that prayer, and meant it, to raise their hands. Randy raised his hand. He turned to his wife, Jennifer, and said, "I've never done that before; I've never been saved." He then walked the aisle, and I led him to Christ. Not long after that night, I had the privilege of baptizing him.

I was not the only one who had been talking to Randy before he walked the aisle to accept Christ. Mike Adams, Jeff Bowman, and Bill Mitchell all took the time to talk to him. Mike Adams, a construction contractor (whom I had led to Jesus earlier), was frequently working on some of the new houses in our neighborhood. Jeff Bowman and his wife, Dena, were also building a house in the subdivision. Bill Mitchell had also started building a house soon after construction had begun on our house.

All of these men and their families were attending Lindsay Lane at the time. We all knew each other, so I introduced Randy and Jennifer to them. As a result, friendships between them began to grow. Randy was now able to see us

---

[28] Murray Wilton was then pastor of Southside Baptist Church in Huntsville, Alabama.
[29] See footnote number 26.

as just a bunch of guys having a good time together, and he wanted what he was seeing in us—a relationships with Jesus Christ.

Once Randy had accepted Christ, God started changing his life. He had a hunger to grow. He was constantly coming to me, asking questions and requesting books that he could study. I gave him the "Survival Kit,"[30] a workbook for new Christians. He completed that study in a very short time, and asked for more. I couldn't believe the way in which he finished the workbooks in such a short time. Randy and Jennifer also joined a Sunday school class, where he continued to grow.

A few years later, Randy was ordained a deacon at Lindsay Lane. He has continued to find new opportunities for service. God has blessed him with the gift of service and with a passion for people.

In 2002, I hired Randy to be the Minister of Assimilation at Lindsay Lane. He is also our Outreach Pastor. His primary role is to help new members get acclimated to the church. Randy meets with each new Christian, or new church member, to begin the process of "plugging" him or her into the church. His is a role that requires both patience and a heart to mentor people.

We ask all of our new members to complete a "Spiritual

---

[30] Latham, Bill and Ralph W. Neighbors, Survival Kit for New Christians (Nashville, TN: LifeWay Christian Resources, 1979).

Gifts Survey." Randy uses these surveys to identify the new members' gifts and talents. As a result, he is able to channel our new members into the various ministries and in meeting the needs within our church.

In only five short years, Randy has gone from planting "preacher hedges" to serving as an ordained minister at Lindsay Lane. He truly has a gift and passion to serve others.

Eddy McLemore

One night, I preached a revival in a Lincoln, Tennessee, church where Elwanda McLemore was attending. A year later, Elwanda started looking for a new church. One Sunday morning, she decided to visit Lindsay Lane. She drove almost thirty miles from her home in Tennessee to attend our services. Elwanda began to attend regularly; I eventually had the privilege of meeting her. Just as I had asked Mike Adam's wife, Tammy, where her husband was, I now asked Elwanda the same question. She gave me the same answer that I had received from Tammy Adams—Eddy McLemore doesn't attend church.

She told me, "He works at the local plant, and is currently laid off. He is having a hard time because he loves to work and do things." She then asked me, "Do you have anything he could do for you at the church? Maybe he could

Sharing My Faith

come here and do something."

I said, "We'll find something for him."

The next day, I went to see Bradley.[31] I asked him if we had any work that needed to be done, because I wanted to get Eddy down there. Bradley told me that, since we had recently moved into our current sanctuary, we needed to have some painting done. I told him that I would ask Eddy to help.

I called Elwanda and told her we had some work for Eddy. Within a few days, Eddy drove down to the church. I introduced myself to him, and introduced him to Bradley. Again, I wanted to first build a relationship with Eddy. I let him know that we were just ordinary folks.

During our first visit, I said to Eddy, "So, your name is McLemore! As soon as I heard your name, I knew you were a good man." He laughed, since he knew that we weren't even closely related. Eddy began to understand that, even though I was a preacher, I was still an okay guy.

Eddy started painting that day. I began building a relationship and a friendship with him. Every day, I would make a point of finding him so we would just talk. We often spoke about what he had done at work.

We eventually discovered that we had played softball on opposing teams. I learned that Eddy knew a couple of my friends; one of them was Stan Holt. This opened a door

---
[31] Bradley Griggs, our Executive Pastor at Lindsay Lane.

to talk about things we had in common: the softball games we had played and the guys on our teams. Just by spending some time together, and talking about our daily lives, we formed a relationship.

One day, when Eddy came to work at the church, I took him to lunch at the local Cracker Barrel™ restaurant. We used this opportunity to continue to get to know each other.

After lunch, Eddy and I returned to the church. While we were still in the parking lot, I asked Eddy for his permission to ask a personal question.

He said, "Sure."

I said, "Eddy, have you ever given your life to Jesus Christ?"

He said, "No, I don't think I've ever really done that."

I then asked, "Eddy, wouldn't you like to do that? You can do it right now."

"No," he said, "I don't want to do that right now."

I replied, "Okay, I just wanted to ask."

We went back inside the church where Eddy continued to work on a growing list of projects.

The following Sunday, Elwanda and I met briefly in the sanctuary. I told her about my conversation with Eddy. She told me that he had mentioned it to her. She said that she was getting excited about the possibility of Eddy accepting Christ.

Sharing My Faith

The next day, Monday, I went to see Bradley again. I asked him, again, to find something for Eddy to do. I then called Eddy; I asked him to come back to the church to work. I tracked him down at lunchtime to ask him to go to lunch a second time with me. I could clearly see that he was under conviction to accept Christ.

When we returned from lunch, I again stopped in the church parking lot. I asked, "Eddy, did you think about what I talked about with you the last time?"

He said, "I sure did."

"Eddy," I asked, "is there any reason that you wouldn't want to ask Jesus Christ to become your Lord and Savior?"

He replied, "No sir, there's not."

I asked, "Eddy, are you ready to do it now?"

His reply, this time, was, "I sure am."

I told Eddy that I could lead him to Christ right there in the truck.

"Well," he said, "I'd like to go in the church under that big old cross. I'd like to accept Christ right there."

We went into the sanctuary, knelt at the cross, and I led him to Christ. He prayed the "Sinner's Prayer"[32] at the cross. And, the next Sunday, I baptized my new friend!

Eddy, like Randy Brown, was another new Christian that grew quickly. He kept coming back to me with questions. And, like Randy, he loves to serve others.

---

[32] See footnote number 26.

Eddy and Elwanda drove every week from Tennessee to attend our services. Within a few years, I had the honor of ordaining him as a deacon at Lindsay Lane.

Eddy formed a group of his friends into what he now calls, the "Wayne Peters Ministry." He named this ministry in honor of one of our church members. After a disabling stroke, Dale Peters asked if anyone would be willing to visit her husband, Wayne, in the nursing home. Eddy and Robert Sturdivant got together, and started visiting with Wayne on a regular basis.

It was during these visits that Eddy realized the enormous need for a nursing home, assisted living, and home visitation ministry. He didn't care if a patient or resident was a member of our church—he visited members and nonmembers alike. Eddy and Robert started introducing themselves at long-term and short-term care facilities.

This ministry now reaches more than two hundred people each week. Eddy and his friends have formed relationships with every person they have visited, and those relationships have continued for years. Hundreds of people's lives have been touched and changed by a man who, once, had no relationship with Jesus Christ!

I began my relationship with all four of these men by talking about something we had in common. It gave each of them the opportunity to see me, not as a preacher, but as a friend—someone who, in many ways, was a lot like them.

I believe the key to witnessing is to first build a relationship. However, it's important to remember that everything happens in God's timing. Often when we witness, because of what He's done in our life, we want others to hurry up and accept Christ. Relationships may form either slowly or quickly—we should never attempt to force it to fit into our time frames. Once you build a relationship with someone, they are more apt to think that, if God has done something for you, maybe He would also do it for them.

God has really blessed me by putting these four guys into my life. They've encouraged me to continue building relationships with lost and unchurched people.

I often think about the time it takes to build and to maintain a relationship. With the exception of Eddy, I came to know these men in my early years at Lindsay Lane. I had more time to focus on relationships than I do today, with all of the demands of being a pastor. Meetings and administrative duties are demanding more of my time today. I have to balance my time with God, my family, and my church in such a way that I do not damage any of these vital relationships. I may be a pastor 24/7, but I've learned to build in some outlets. It wasn't easy learning this lesson—I had to learn it from others.

In the early years of growing our church, I was giving

more time to the church than I was giving to my family. My wife was becoming jealous of the church—she felt that Lindsay Lane was becoming my "bride." I wasn't respecting her wishes for me to spend time with her and with our two daughters.

I've now built in the outlets. I have set my work schedule to include time for God and for my family.

One of the things I've learned is to have an "off day." Fridays are now set aside for my family—and for me. I play golf, work in the yard, visit my Mom and Dad, or do anything that helps me to relax. That's how I regroup, and it's revolutionized my ministry.

My mentor, Johnny Hunt, taught me to plan "date times" with Patsy. He told me that a busy pastor needs margins—built in for time— with his wife and with his family. He taught me to do something special for them at least once every few months.

One thing I like is to do is to go on mission trips with Patsy. It's something I really enjoy, because we're able to share the experiences together.

Recently, our church implemented a plan for each of the senior pastors at Lindsay Lane to take sabbaticals. For every five years a pastor serves at Lindsay Lane, he receives one week off for a sabbatical. These sabbaticals are times intended for the pastors and their spouses to refresh them, renew them, and give them time for reflection.

For my twentieth year at Lindsay Lane, Patsy and I were given a four-week sabbatical. It was truly a gift from God. It helped us both immensely. The sabbatical had such a visible effect on me that two of our older ladies came to me. They said:

> *You know what? That sabbatical has changed your preaching. We think you should take off every July. We can tell how much it has helped you to be refreshed.*

As a pastor, I get emotionally involved in the lives of people—in times of sadness and in times of joy. So that I can effectively help others, I occasionally need to take a few days off. It does no one any good when their pastor works himself into an emotional fatigue. This is how pastors burn out. They forget the fact that they are only human. They also need outlets so that they can remain useful and joyful servants.

I've been most fortunate that I have been able to exercise regularly. I have also gone on several mission trips. Although, I didn't realize it at first, these mission trips have helped me to get away from the stresses of my daily tasks.

I've realized that I need to plan times to get away. In fact, two years ago, I went through a period of time when I had no drive to be creative or to exert myself. I could not understand why I was so tired. I didn't have the passion for the church that I once had. Since then, I've learned that I need to build margins into my ministerial life.

I truly love being a pastor. And I also love my wife, my family, my friends, and my church. In order to keep this focus and passion, I need to be willing to admit that I'm human. Like everyone else, I need rest and times for being refreshed. And, as I have discovered, I often need those times even more than others.

TEN

The Lindsay Lane Vision

"Vision" may be defined as, "being able to visualize something before you can actually see the results." Furthermore, it is "having the gift of leading others to see the same revelation that God has revealed to you." As I have previously mentioned in this book, the most profound definition I've ever heard of vision is, "If you don't see it before you see it, you'll never see it!"[33]

Although Lindsay Lane is truly a marvelous church, we still need to be continuously challenged. If we aren't, the church will slowly drift into a state of complacency. I often remind our church members that we need to constantly be witnesses. We must share both our vision and our faith with others. That, in a nutshell, is exactly why Lindsay Lane has grown into the church that it is today.

The vision of Lindsay Lane actually began in September of 1988, when Pastor Phil Daws planted the church.

---

[33] Dr. Johnny Hunt's definition, found in Chapter Eight: Called Out by God.

When Phil left the church in 1990, the church called Phillip Schrimsher to be their new pastor. Phillip had the gift of evangelism and the heart of an evangelist; he, therefore, only stayed one year at Lindsay Lane.

At that time, Dr. Phineas Earle Trent accepted the call to become their interim pastor. Dr. Trent was a godly saint of a man (like Moses), and a very seasoned pastor! He had previously pastored several churches, and was currently the director of missions in nearby Lauderdale County.[34]

When the church called me to become their new bivocational pastor in April of 1992, Dr. Trent was in the hospital. Upon my arrival at Lindsay Lane, I was told that Brother Trent[35] was in critical condition at the Athens-Limestone Hospital. His condition had become so serious that the doctors had called his family to tell them to come quickly to the hospital.

Anticipating the worst, I joined with the Trent family at the hospital. Brother Trent, however, made a miraculous recovery. For a while, we laughingly deemed him, "Lazarus"[36] (this happened on a couple of other occasions; each time he would bounce back)!

In the early months of my pastorate at Lindsay Lane, Brother Trent was still able to drive to church in his Cadillac. Eventually, however, the family took his keys away

---

[34] The associational camp there still bears his name: the "Earle Trent Assembly."

[35] As he was known at Lindsay Lane. [36] John 11:43.

from him; he was no longer permitted to drive for himself. His solution? He hired five different chauffeurs to drive him around! The reason that he chose to hire five drivers was to make sure that someone would always be available when he needed to go somewhere.

On Sunday mornings and Sunday nights, I would personally pick Brother Trent up to bring him to church. For me, this was time well spent—it gave us some quality time so we could talk. He would always share some gold nuggets about church life, or about his early years as a pastor. To me, those five-mile conversations were like sitting in a seminary professor's class!

In those early days, Dr. Trent taught me about the need to have a vision. Lindsay Lane was growing. As a result, we were quickly running out of educational space. Brother Trent sent a letter of application to the Alabama Baptist State Convention on our behalf, requesting that they would send us a mobile unit.[37] Brother Trent wrote, "Lindsay Lane Baptist Church has a new pastor who is leading our church into what, I believe, will be the next Whitesburg."[38]

I remember thinking, "How in the world can he possibly believe that Lindsay Lane could ever grow into that large of a church?" The answer: Brother Trent had a vision! I would later learn to catch that same vision.

---

[37] A trailer that is temporarily used for educational space.
[38] At that time, Whitesburg Baptist Church in Huntsville, AL, had close to three thousand members; Lindsay Lane only had about sixty!

It began with a simple slogan that Brother Trent coined to increase our Sunday school attendance. He said to me, "Let's see if we can grow to 92 in '92."[39] I gasped! "Ninety-two? We only have fifty or sixty people coming to our church! I don't know if we can possibly reach that many in a Sunday morning worship service."

Brother Trent responded simply, and with confidence, "I'm not talking about a worship service—I'm talking about ninety-two in Sunday school. I think we can reach that many by the end of this year."

He pronounced his vision for that goal at some point in July of 1992. I was somewhat shocked. I really couldn't believe it. So I told him, "Well, we'll see what we can do." We erected a banner that read, "92 in '92." We challenged our people to invite others and to trust God to honor our vision. I was thinking to myself, "Yeah, right!"

We hung Brother Trent's visionary slogan right over the pulpit. I began preaching messages on the vision of reaching 92 in '92! That's when God began to stir my heart; I, too, began to catch the vision that I was trying to convince others to adopt!

We had set the date to fulfill the goal for the last Sunday in December of 1992. Would you believe that, on that very morning, Athens was hit with a severe ice storm? Early that morning I stood there, alone, in the church parking lot. I

---

[39] 92 people in attendance by the year 1992.

The Lindsay Lane Vision

became angry with God! I thought, "God, what are You doing? We've been trying to reach this high attendance goal. Our people have been praying earnestly for it. I've been challenging the congregation. How could You let this ice storm happen?"

I had already called Beth Malady, a lady from Whitesburg Baptist Church. She was scheduled to present our special music that morning. I told her that, because of the ice, she didn't need to come to the church. She replied, "No, I'm coming. I think I can make it."

I continued to stand there, alone, in the parking lot. I was sulking when, suddenly, cars began driving in—one car after another turned into our parking lot.

That morning, the last Sunday of December of 1992, we had one hundred and ten people attend Sunday school! Unbelievable! What a miracle of God! My God was teaching me a valuable lesson that I have never forgotten!

God's Holy Spirit spoke to my heart that day. He said: "Big boy, you just let me run the show! All I want for you to do is to trust Me, and to follow Me from now on." And I have!

That Sunday morning I finally learned the principal of having a vision! God showed me, first hand, that if I would trust Him, believe in Him, and let Him do great and mighty things, He would reveal His strong hand. He responds to the faith of His people.

From that point forward, I have continued to challenge our people on many occasions to believe and trust the hand of God. But, because of the events of that day, I now have total confidence and faith in Him!

Lindsay Lane's growth continued. We quickly reached a point at which we needed more room for classes. God gave me a vision to build an Education Building to help accommodate our Sunday school growth. One night, around 11:00 p.m., I sat down and drew up the plans that we would later utilize for building our new educational facilities. This new addition was estimated to cost $250,000—a huge price tag for a church of 100 or so people! But our small congregation was catching the vision of how God could "do great and mighty things that we never knew!" We soon adopted Jeremiah 33:3 as our church's motto! Our congregation began a period of rapid growth, because the people of Lindsay Lane were simply trusting in God to lead us!

One of my fondest memories during this time was when two older gentlemen, Bill Holt and Carlos Blackwell, came to Lindsay Lane. Bill and Carlos were old friends, and longtime drinking buddies. One Sunday morning, when I gave the invitation, they came down the aisle—holding hands! They would later tell me that one of them had said to the other, "I'll go if you'll go." They were both gloriously saved that day! I would have the privilege of baptizing both of them. Soon afterward, however, I preached at both of their funerals.

In the summer of 1996, we began building our second sanctuary. The Carpenters for Christ team from my brother's church in Birmingham, AL, came. They helped us to build a new five hundred-seat sanctuary. What a glorious time! My brother had not only mentored me in the early days after my call to preach—he was now sharing this time of victory with me!

Because of continued growth, we were only in the new sanctuary for six months before we needed to go to two worship services. To God be the glory! We witnessed many people being saved during this period.

One of those people was Scott Sandy! Many church members had been praying for Scott to be saved. It was the Sunday when we were celebrating the completion of the new sanctuary with the Carpenters for Christ Group. I remember that we had a packed house that Sunday! Right before the invitation, I thought, to myself, "No one will probably respond today. It's just too crowded this morning." To my surprise, I soon saw Scott come walking down the aisle. He sincerely accepted Jesus Christ as his Savior.

His mother-in-law, Diane Ernest, was the church pianist.

As Scott came down the aisle, Diane quit playing the piano. She shouted for joy. Scott Sandy was gloriously saved that day!

God just kept revealing Himself to us in a powerful way, and our vision for Lindsay Lane continued to grow. By 1998, we desperately needed a Family Life Center. So we built a nice gymnasium, complete with a commercial kitchen and a spacious loft above.

This facility has been greatly utilized throughout the years for all sorts of activities. We now use it for Sunday school space, luncheons, birthday parties, family socials, Upward basketball games, and a variety of other events that allow our fellow Christians to gather.

In the year 2000, we witnessed continued growth of the number of young families in our church, so we added a very nice children's wing to our growing campus.

Lindsay Lane was now offering two worship services and two Sunday schools, both of which were experiencing exponential growth! At that time, I felt that God was leading me to begin the early stages of casting a vision for a new sanctuary. While finalizing a Capital Stewardship Campaign, I conveyed to the church members that we weren't building this new sanctuary for those of us who were already attending Lindsay Lane. Rather, the new sanctuary would provide the space we would need to accommodate the many people

The Lindsay Lane Vision

who would eventually join our fellowship!

Our sanctuary was full in both services; we had nowhere else to put our new people. I knew that God would continue to bless us with additional growth if we would only believe in, and follow, Him.

And God did bless us! In December 2002, we moved into our new seventeen hundred seat sanctuary. I asked my dear friend and mentor, Dr. Johnny Hunt, if he would come and preach during our dedication service. At that time, we had seven hundred members; the seating capacity of the new sanctuary was seventeen hundred. It would not be long before we would add a second Sunday morning service! These were extremely exciting times at Lindsay Lane, as many souls were being saved for the kingdom of God! God was richly and gloriously blessing His church!

The last thing on my mind during this time was the prospect of building another facility! But God was adding many new people to our fellowship, most of which were young couples with children. It was during this time that God began to greatly speak to my heart concerning the next generation of young kids—those that were coming behind us!

I began to seek the Lord about how Lindsay Lane could truly make a difference in the lives of these young people. I couldn't stop thinking about our children. In previous years, God had given me a vision for organizing a Christian school at Lindsay Lane. The idea had resonated in the back of my heart for many years—almost twelve years or so.

Dr. Wayne Forsythe was organizing a school in our area that he called "Faith Christian Academy." I remember that he approached me for the purpose of asking me to host a town hall meeting at Lindsay Lane. He wanted to explain his vision to the community.

Later, Faith Academy built their school in our area. We at Lindsay Lane supported the school wholeheartedly. We sent interested church members to help organize it.

I began thinking that it would be great if our church had its own Christian academy. I truly believed that our church members would support a Christian school. So, even then, the vision of Lindsay Lane Christian Academy (henceforth, LLCA) was beginning to form in my heart.

My heart's desire was to train our young people to become faithful followers of Jesus Christ. If we would teach our children and youth to become disciples of Christ, we could reach the next generation for the kingdom of heaven! Our children have a tremendous need to develop a strong, Christian worldview. The foundation we could lay through a Christian academy would help them to face a world in which they will, one day, become the parents and the leaders!

Our children's programs were all growing. We were

The Lindsay Lane Vision

quickly running out of space for the children. On Sunday nights, for example, our AWANA classes were meeting in storage closets and out in the hallways. We simply had no more space available for our children.

So, in 2007, I began to cast the vision to the members of Lindsay Lane Church to pray about constructing a Children's Building. I went before the congregation to ask for their support. We began construction in 2007 and, later, moved into the new, state-of-the-art, children's facility in the fall of 2008—a large, 42,000 square feet, edifice.

But the vision and the purpose for the project were the most important ingredients: this facility would house our next generation of young people! This is where we, as a church, could invest in the training and nurturing of many young people for Christ! A portion of this very nice facility was also destined to become the future home of LLCA, an incubator where we could raise up Champions for Christ! The vision God had given me twelve years before was now coming to fruition! Again, God was at work!

A long awaited vision was realized in 2009, when we opened the LLCA. We began with thirty-nine students in kindergarten through the sixth grade. We added a seventh grade class in our second year. We were unable to pursue, however, any additional grades within the confines of our limited space.

Then, in 2011, God opened a huge door of opportunity for our Christian school! As a sign of God's affirmation and confirmation that He wanted Lindsay Lane Church to have a Christian Academy, something very miraculous happened—the facilities from the "Faith Christian Academy" were now being offered to Lindsay Lane Church for us to purchase![40] God had richly blessed us with what we had sincerely been praying for! LLCA could now offer K-3 through twelfth grade! We found ourselves with 283 students located on three separate campuses! LLCA was formed and the vision had been fulfilled! Only an awesome God could do such a thing!

I am currently praying, and seeking the Lord, for the purpose of acquiring extra land to consolidate LLCA. We could build a new high school and move the Academy onto one campus.

God is, once again, at work. He has already fulfilled another vision by sending us a new Headmaster for LLCA. Our enrollment has also grown steadily to a total of 350 students! To God be the glory, great things He has done!

Allow me to share a word of personal testimony concerning vision. From the moment I was saved in 1979, I've had a deep conviction regarding the security of my relationship with Jesus Christ. My faith has never diminished. It may be difficult for some to believe, but I have never doubt-

---

[40] The Academy that had been proposed to the public years previously during the special town hall meeting at Lindsay Lane Church.

ed either my salvation or God's redemption of my life! His grace was freely given to me on that dark October night. This is most significant, because I have experienced my salvation and vision for Lindsay Lane in much the same way. I don't take lightly the many changes and the growth we have enjoyed at Lindsay Lane.

When I write or speak about vision, it is only after a time of sincere prayer and truly seeking God's direction and His will. To me, a vision is not just a good idea or a well-thought out plan. A vision can only come from God while we are seeking His heart and His will.

As leaders, we can expect many different types of reactions when casting a vision. There will always be critics and naysayers, because many people will just flat-out resist change! That's why the vision must be sincerely prayed over and clearly presented. Knowing that vision will involve change, there's always the chance of losing some good friends—and a few church members, too! But, on the other hand, there's also the chance of gaining some new friends and church members through vision as well.

I've found that most people are attracted to churches that embrace a vision of reaching the world for Christ. When leading a congregation to catch the vision, leaders must be firm in their obedience to God. They must have the assurance of their callings. They must know, in their hearts, that the vision is from God—and not from their own personal desires or imaginations! That's essential!

Communication is the essential key in casting a vision! Many pastors have visions, but do not clearly communicate their visions to their people. A congregation needs to know and understand the vision, as well as the heart, of their leader. Habakkuk says to "write the vision down."[41]

By the way, I did just that in my first six months as the pastor of Lindsay Lane! I still have the handwritten paper on which I wrote the vision and presented it to the congregation in 1992! When the pastor's vision becomes the people's vision, then you're ready to move forward. If people do not catch the vision, or don't clearly understand or support the vision, then you can expect major problems. Oftentimes, it may not be that the people resist the vision, but rather they just don't fully understand or comprehend it. There are times when you may have to clarify and repeat the vision again and again. Some people just need more time to pray about, and dissect, the vision in order to support it. Remember: the pastor has had more time to pray about, and embrace, the vision. So, be patient in casting the vision so that others can have ample time to do the same.

One vision that has "become sight" for those of us at Lindsay Lane has been in the area of missions. Our Lord Jesus exhorts us in the Great Commission:[42]

---

[41] Habakkuk 2:2. [42] Matthew 28:19-20.

Go therefore and make disciples of all the nations, baptizing them in the name of the Father and of the Son and of the Holy Spirit, teaching them to observe all things that I have commanded you; and lo, I am with you always, even to the end of the age.

When I first arrived at Lindsay Lane in 1992, I knew very little about missions. I had neither been trained about the need to be personally involved, nor had I ever taught others about missions. Much less, I had never been on a mission trip.

In 1997 a pastor friend, John Garrison, invited me to go with him on a mission trip to Zambia, Africa. This trip completely changed how I viewed missions. It greatly opened the eyes of my understanding as to just how people live in other countries. Our journey took us deeply into the Zambian bush country, far away from the modern conveniences of American life.

I really admired the Zambians for their love of Jesus Christ. I was amazed by the fact that they had no idea why someone would consider them to be "poor." It was in the bush of Africa that I witnessed the phenomenon of the Zambian people actually shedding tears because we had run out of Bibles; sadly, some were unable to get one.

Upon my return from Africa, I began to teach and share my passion for missions! There were a couple of families in our church that had been previously involved on mission trips. And so, with the help and leadership of the Snider and Colella families, we began our involvement with missions by starting a new block party ministry.

We took a group of our people to set up the parties in various neighborhoods. We gathered the crowds using music, puppets, testimonies and, of course, food! We then used skits to share the message of the Gospel. Then I, or someone else, preached the Word.

Enthusiasm and excitement concerning missions were soon spreading throughout our church. Before long, we were able to lead our church members to catch the vision of growing and going. We were reaching the nations through involvement in missions. One-by-one, more members were joining with us on the mission trips. The not-so-surprising result? When we took more mission trips, we produced more missionaries.

The greatest rewards for our efforts in missions have been the long-term relationships we've established with missions organizations and our evolving partnerships with missionaries. Our Lindsay Lane church members have now gone on mission trips to several countries—and almost every continent. Lindsay Lane is now very missions-minded, because people have caught the vision! Many of our members' lives have been radically changed and transformed as they have

The Lindsay Lane Vision

joined with our Lord on these mission trips. They have seen, firsthand, God's hand at work! And it has all happened as the result of our casting a vision for missions!

As I write this book, my vision of launching a new church plant is also coming to fruition! On November 3, 2013, we're launching a new church in nearby Harvest, Alabama. Our College and Student Pastor, Andy John King, and his core team will lead it. We believe that the new church campus, Lindsay Lane East, will grow quickly, making an immediate impact for the kingdom of God!

Again, God is honoring a much-prayed-over vision of reaching people with the Gospel of Jesus Christ! As the senior pastor of such an awesome church, I'm grateful to God that our people are catching this vision.

Yes, my dear friends, vision is extremely vital and essential to any church or organization. The Bible states, "Where there is no revelation (vision) the people perish."[43] Rick Warren paraphrased this verse when he said, "Where there's no vision, the people will find a new *parish*!"

My prayer for Lindsay Lane is that God will continue the vision that He started there twenty-five years ago!

---

[43] Proverbs 29:18.

ELEVEN

Worship, Serve, Grow

Our purpose statement at Lindsay Lane is, "Making disciples who worship, grow, and serve." Being a *disciple* of the Lord Jesus Christ simply means we are *followers* of Jesus. We imitate Christ by observing His life. We imitate what He has done by learning about His character. We then ask for His help as we develop that character into our own lives.

We become disciple-makers as well. The truths that we have personally gleaned as disciples we're now able to pass on to others. Therefore, it's important for us to learn how disciple one another.

To reiterate, at Lindsay Lane, we're trying to make disciples. Our purpose statement, therefore, simply states, "Making disciples who worship, grow, and serve."

Early in my Christian life, right after I was saved, I realized that I needed to grow in Christ. I needed to be mentored in order to become a disciple of the Lord Jesus Christ. I wanted to follow Jesus. I wanted to learn about Him, and I wanted to grow in Him. I was discipled by others in the Lord, and so I began to grow in my relationship with the Lord Jesus Christ. I knew that I had received Christ's grace and mercy. I learned that He loved me and, as a result, I wanted to be an example to others. So I made the decision to grow spiritually and to develop discipline in my life.

Our purpose statement—to make disciples who worship the Lord—truly reflects how I really love to worship God. The Bible says in Psalm 45:11, "Because He is your Lord; worship Him." This word, "worship," simply means that we give Him our adoration and praise. I really do love praising and worshiping my God.

As a disciple who is seeking to follow my Lord Jesus Christ, I am to worship Him in spirit and truth. I worship Him as my Savior and my God. I worship Him in the truth of His Word. Through song, I am able to worship Him, and to give Him adoration from my heart and lips as I praise Him.

A disciple not only needs to learn how to worship, but he or she also needs to learn how to grow in Jesus Christ. We grow in many ways: by reading His Word, by prayer, and by being discipled by others. It is imperative, therefore, that we find someone who can disciple us, mentor us, and help us grow in the Lord. "Growth" simply means that we fall in love with the Lord Jesus Christ and with His Word.

A Christian must then learn to discipline himself or herself. He or she must set priorities in his or her life, because there will be many distractions.

The devil will make sure that you will be distracted. He's going to put a lot of obstacles, including good things, into your path to keep you from the main thing.

Do you remember the story of Mary and Martha? Martha was distracted by doing many things, while Mary concentrated on the main thing: worshiping God.

Mary and Martha are good examples of how to serve and worship God. And we need people who are like both of them in our church. We need many Marthas to focus on serving others and meeting the needs of people. We also need many Marys, people who will concentrate on improving their personal spiritual walks with Christ.

Paul wrote, "I discipline my body and bring it into subjection, lest, when I have preached to others, I myself should become disqualified."[44] Note the word "discipline." As disciples of Christ, we grow through discipline. As we grow through discipline, we will become more like Jesus Christ. We must learn to "die to self." According to S. Michael Houdmann:[45]

---

[44] 1 Corinthians 9:27. [45] http://www.gotquestions.org/dying-to-self.html, site visited on 1/30/2014.

> *The concept of "dying to self" is found throughout the New Testament. It expresses the true essence of the Christian life, in which we take up our cross and follow Christ. Dying to self is part of being born again; the old self dies and the new self comes to life (John 3:3–7). Not only are Christians born again when we come to salvation, but we also continue dying to self as part of the process of sanctification. As such, dying to self is both a one-time event and a lifelong process.*

For the Christian, "dying to self" is imperative. John the Baptist said, "He must increase, but I must decrease."[46] The apostle Paul also knew that. He said [my paraphrase], "My life in the flesh needs to die. I need to die to self so that I might live for Christ." He wrote:

> *I have been crucified with Christ; it is no longer I who live, but Christ lives in me; and the life which I now live in the flesh I live by faith in the Son of God, who loved me and gave Himself for me.*

Paul knew that the key to being a disciple was learning to die to self and live for Christ. That takes discipline—daily discipline—to follow Him. Jesus said, "If you're going to be my disciple you must learn to pick up your cross and follow me daily."[47]

As a disciple of Christ, I need to learn to worship and

---

[46] John 3:30. [47] Mark 10:21.

grow in Him. As I discipline my life, I will become more like Christ. The result of this discipline will be that I will fall in love with Christ. He will give me the desire, or passion, to follow Him and become more like Him.

James Merritt, lead pastor of Cross Pointe Church in Duluth, Georgia, once said, "We can have as much of God and His Word as we want." That's a true statement.

Even in my marriage, I can have as much of a relationship with Patsy as I want. I can be as close to her as I want, but it will take discipline to let go of other distractions so that I can focus on my wife.

My walk with the Lord is similar to my relationship with Patsy. I can get as close to Him as I want—through prayer and reading His Word. However, I must discipline myself if I want to get closer and closer to my God.

I loved my wife when I married her. But, after forty years of marriage, I now *really* love her. The Bible says that. "Two shall become as one."[48] In our forty years of marriage, Patsy and I have really, really become as one. After forty years with her, I have learned which buttons to push—and which buttons *not* to push.

In my walk with Christ, I've grown closer to Him. I've disciplined myself in my walk with Him. I personally believe that my spiritual growth has been greatly aided both by my reading of God's Word and by my worship of Him.

---

[48] Ephesians 5:31.

Many people along the way have also greatly helped me to grow in Christ. Being a part of a great church has aided me, too.

We will all face trials and tribulations, and will experience many difficulties along our life's journey. If we will stay close to Christ, He will help us. One way that He will use to help us is through the various support groups within the church. I believe the entire church is to be our support group. Small groups inside the church, such as Sunday school classes and various ministries, will also help us to grow as Christians. These small groups can help to disciple and nurture us as Christians.

I will never forget my first Sunday school class at Round Island Baptist Church where I grew up. As I have previously written, someone in that class gave me my first Bible.[49] They placed it on an empty chair—a chair that they had set aside specifically for me. The members of that Sunday school class taught me about Jesus, and discipled me in my early walk with Christ.

We all need the church, and we all need to be discipled by individuals and small groups that will support us in our spiritual growth. No man is an island. As the Bible says, "Iron sharpens iron."[50]

Jesus instructed us to pray for each other because we need each other. The church comes alongside each of us.

---

[49] See Chapter Six: "Round Island—My Seminary." [50] Proverbs 27:17.

It strengthens us in the areas in which we are weak. I know, personally, that my church has greatly strengthened me over the years.

Someone every one of us needs is a mentor. We all need that person (or persons) that can sharpen us, strengthen us, pray for us, come alongside of us, and help us grow as Christians.

Paul was a mentor to many, especially to young Timothy. He called Timothy, "a son in the ministry."[51] Paul wrote, "Imitate me, just as I also imitate Christ."[52]

Many people have helped to disciple and mentor me along my personal journey. One of the greatest mentors in my life has been Dr. Johnny Hunt. He has greatly helped me over the years to develop my personal walk with my Lord, Jesus Christ. I've attended many of his "Timothy–Barnabas" retreats and conferences.[53] He has taken me on as both a friend and as a fellow laborer in the vineyard. He has discipled me and mentored me for years. I love him for that. I will never be able to repay him for the time and effort he has invested in mentoring me.

My brother, Mike, has also mentored me—both one-on-one directly and by proxy. I have watched his life. I have seen how God has greatly enriched him and helped him in his ministry. I've gleaned many things from him and, from time-to-time, he has poured his life into mine.

---

[51] 1 Timothy 1:2. [52] 1 Corinthians 11:1.
[53] http://timothybarnabas.org/

Dr. Earle Trent, the interim pastor when I arrived at Lindsay Lane, was another of my mentors. An older gentleman, reminiscent of Moses, he instructed me as we walked side-by-side in those early days. Dr. Trent took me, a young, green pastor, and mentored me into an experienced pastor and a true Christian leader.

As disciples of Christ, we all need to learn to worship Him. We also need to grow. Thirdly, we need to serve. Jesus Christ said that He didn't come to *be served*—He came to *serve*.[54]

I believe that service produces growth, and growth will also result in service. One who loves the Lord will want to serve the Lord. As you grow in the Lord, you will grow in His service. That service, again, will help you to grow in the Lord.

I thank my parents who, while I was a young boy, daily laid out chores for my brother, my sister, and me to complete. My Mom, especially, made sure every day that we would have responsibilities to carry out. As a pastor today, I recognize how that same work ethic that they instilled in me has helped me so much.

From the moment I was saved, I wanted to be a disciple. I began to grow in the Lord. I took on many responsibilities at Round Island, from singing in the choir to serving as a deacon. I did not realize it back then, but I can now see

---
[54] Matthew 20:28.

how much those responsibilities helped me to grow in my walk with Christ.

I became a servant of Christ and I became His disciple. Christ has given me the gifts of service and encouragement. As the pastor of Lindsay Lane, I am so grateful that there are so many servants and volunteers who are willing to do whatever it takes to minister to, and to serve, others.

In order to be a faithful follower of Jesus Christ, you must first become a disciple. To be a disciple, you must learn to worship our Lord genuinely in your heart. You must learn to grow in your personal relationship with the Lord Jesus Christ. You must learn to die to self—you must decrease so that He may increase. And then, finally, you must learn to be a faithful follower of the Lord Jesus Christ, and to serve Him, His church, and others wholeheartedly—with passion and commitment.

We, as disciples of Christ, have a purpose for our lives. That purpose, at Lindsay Lane, is to make disciples of Christ who will worship, grow and serve.

And so, as your fellow disciple of Christ, I'm thankful for all those who have invested in *my* life. They have helped me along my life's journey to learn to worship, to grow, and to serve.

Epilogue

In writing the story of my life, I have been caused both to reflect and remember just how precious my Lord's grace and mercy truly are! Like the prophet Jonah, I had ignored all the warning signs of a gracious God! I was raised to know about God and His church, but I was never taught about having a personal relationship with God. When the devil came calling, I quickly abandoned my religion. I embraced all the pleasures this world had to offer. Eventually, I found myself in the hopper of sin, in the bottomless pit of despair. My sin had caused me to "Gamble with Eternity!" This book will give you insight, dear reader, into the divine nature of God's mercy, grace, and forgiveness—to anyone, and everyone, who will call upon His name.[55]

Whether you have been "Gambling with Eternity," or you have been on a relatively firm foundation, you need the Lord! My earnest prayer is that this testimonial book will open the eyes of those "whose minds the god of this age has blinded, who do not believe,"[56] and of those who also who feel comfortable in their religiosity—as did the Pharisees. For when you truly meet Jesus, the Savior, your life will be transformed into a new creation.[57] Nothing will matter more in this life than an intimate relationship with Jesus Christ.

At the age of twenty-seven, I finally realized that God loved me more than anyone else ever could—even more

---

[55] Romans 10:13. [56] 2 Corinthians 4:4. [57] 2 Corinthians 5:17.

than I loved myself. As someone said so well, "Jesus is all we will ever need, but we won't realize it until He is all we have." And, my friends, when you're lying at the bottom and you have spent all you have, Jesus is all you will have left! But the Good News is—He is all you ever really needed! Like the Prodigal Son, and the Prophet Jonah, only God can snatch your life from the pit and gloriously transform you from a prodigal to a preacher!

- Dusty McLemore

BIBLIOGRAPHY

Corrie ten Boom, John Sherrill, and
    Elizabeth Sherrill. <u>The Hiding Place</u>
(Old Tappan, NJ: Fleming H. Revell Co., 1974).

Bill Latham and Ralph W. Neighbors. <u>Survival Kit for New Christians </u>(Nashville, TN: LifeWay Christian Resources, 1979).

Made in the USA
Columbia, SC
17 September 2017